Get Serious About
EDITORIAL MANAGEMENT

For Business-to-Business
Media Professionals

Howard S. Rauch

ReefNet Press

Get Serious About Editorial Management

By Howard S. Rauch

Published by: ReefNet Press, Los Angeles

ISBN-10: 1546671390
ISBN-13: 978-1546671398
Printed in USA

Contents

GET SERIOUS ABOUT EDITORIAL MANAGEMENT

INTRODUCTION

L ooking over the front page of a *New York Times* Sunday edition recently, my wife declared in mock dismay, "I'm going to have to read every article in this paper!"

"Really?" I responded astutely. "How come?"

Rather than answering directly, she issued this challenge: "You're supposedly a publishing guru. You tell me."

Knowingly or not, she had touched a raw nerve that could have led to hours of conversation. But my answer was a simple one: "They are probably all exclusives—stories you won't find elsewhere. And most likely the writers reached out to plenty of authoritative sources."

That exchange may have an unpleasant ring for many editors in business-to-business (B2B) media. Increasingly, many of us can't make a similar claim about the must-read nature of our publications. Especially when it comes to online news content, compelling and exclusive reporting is a foreign language for many B2B staffs. Far too much B2B content these days is based on press releases and other rewritten material.

At first glance, this shortcoming might appear to be a journalism problem. But if staff writers are not provided with the resources to produce a greater array of exclusive material, the remedy requires management capability. In fact, many highly skilled editors I know shudder at the thought of assuming a management role.

If you see yourself in that category—that is, if you prefer a job totally devoted to journalism assignments—this book may not be for you. But if you want to have a bigger and longer-lived impact on your publications (and if you want to expand your career options), you will need to develop or enhance your editorial management skills. If you are in this category, read on.

The appeal of editorial management

Perhaps the way I navigated the B2B career ladder may explain how I gradually found the management mode appealing. In pre-college life, I always enjoyed writing projects. When it came time for college, I was still insisting writing was the life for me. But my mother would have preferred accounting. So she put me through an aptitude test battery that showed—much to my satisfaction—that writing was a strong career possibility.

But writing what? That was the question. My test administrator warned me that if I pursued writing as a career, I would surely end up starving and living in an attic. That was none too appealing. The administrator offered a solution: major in advertising—which I did.

On graduating from college, I had two offers—one from a book company paying $62 a week, the other from a radio/TV rep firm paying $65 a week. So of course I went with the higher-paying job. My duties at the new firm included operating the company switchboard. It was an absolute disaster.

But my fortunes soon started to brighten. A colleague who was actively looking to change jobs told me of an opening I might prefer as an assistant editor at a trade publishing company. I had no idea what "trade publishing" meant, but I reasoned that it had to be better than my switchboard duties. So in 1959, I began my B2B career as an assistant editor covering variety stores and restaurants for Lebhar-Friedman's *Chain Store Age* group.

At this early stage of my career, three experiences helped shape my future priorities as an editorial manager.

To begin with, the job interview included a written test based on a field trip. I had to visit a variety store and then write an article based on interesting merchandising trends I observed. Thanks to experience I had working my way through college as a stock boy in a department store's "fourth basement" (don't ask), I was at home in the test environment and landed the job. In my later management years, I frequently used the field visit as part of the screening process when interviewing prospective employees.

My second key experience as an assistant editor was realizing the importance of travel. I was required to constantly visit stores, talking to managers, and photographing interesting displays. It sunk in pretty quickly that without these field trips, you could not really know your industry.

My third key experience was learning that having multiple skills as an editor hugely boosts the chances of your success. Shortly after joining Lebhar-Friedman, I was promoted to a desk editor job on the restaurant edition that eventually became the powerhouse known as *Nation's Restaurant News*. My job involved copyediting and layout. I already found business magazine writing to be a challenge; the prospect of doing layout was absolutely daunting. But I had a great teacher. He had lots of patience with my bungling. Within a few months, I discovered that, for whatever the reason, I had an eye for graphics and was soon laying out and pasting up (remember paste-up?) most of the magazine.

In later years, I met many editors who never had graphics exposure. These editors were satisfied in jobs that were 100-percent writing. So they wore one hat well, but that was the end of it in terms of potential growth: they lost out on management opportunities.

Meanwhile, my teacher at the restaurant edition imbued in me the importance of being willing to train others, a principle I bought into for life. Later on in this book, you will read about my hour-a-day approach to training new recruits. Even when my staff consisted of just one assistant, I felt that during the first 10 days on the job, an entry-level recruit was entitled to at least one-hour of classroom-like conference.

Try that approach sometime. It really works!

In my next job at the newsletter division of Prentice Hall, a book publisher, I learned much about developing how-to management and marketing articles. Here I learned that if an article was well researched, readers would follow the advice described, improve their businesses, and offer feedback on the value of the article. This experience drummed into me the importance of including how-to content in editorial line-ups, no matter what industry is covered.

After Prentice Hall, I made a brief stop in a PR position that didn't appeal, then tried freelancing. One of my clients— *Vending Times*—offered me a managing editor position, and I jumped at the chance. The vending machine industry was fascinating; news about selling products from a coin-operated machine was non-stop.

Back then, *VT* was a small operation turning out a monthly 16-page tabloid. But the publisher had big plans. He knew the industry well and the industry knew him. He was big on travel, and at one point I spent eight consecutive weekends covering regional association meetings.

The experience reinforced for me what I had learned as an assistant editor about the importance of travel. I became acquainted with people all over the country, had dinner with them and their families, and we got to know each other as friends rather than editor and source. I stayed at *VT* for four great years as the publication grew from number three in its market to the top spot.

My next stop was with Gralla Publications, where I stayed for 21 years. Landing this job was an exercise in serendipity. One weekend in 1968 I just had an overwhelming urge to move on and answered every suitable want ad in the *New York Times*. A Gralla executive responded and invited me to visit. Before my interview, I researched the company. It had four magazines serving contract decorating, kitchen & bath installation, multi-housing building and banking equipment.

The fields held no appeal, but I figured maybe the visit would change my mind.

As it turned out, the opening involved a start-up in the sporting goods retail market. My reaction when I was shown the dummy for the first issue was, wow! I landed the position as editor/associate publisher in 1968. Over the next several years, I moved up to group editor before being named vice president/editorial director in 1976. At that time, we were launching our 12th magazine. We continued to grow rapidly, and by 1989, I was supervising over 100 journalists with regional offices located in Chicago, Los Angeles, and Dallas.

Lessons learned

Gralla's top management, Milt and Lawrence Gralla, were journalists by background. They placed great store in editorial quality. It was a great place to work and I was encouraged to develop a variety of management programs that became specializations when I eventually became a consultant in 1989.

My favorite accomplishment at Gralla was creating one of the most extensive in-house editorial training programs in the business magazine field. At its peak, the program held more than 40 workshops a year geared to various junior or senior editorial management levels. Many people in the industry knew of my in-house program and were eager to launch something similar in their organizations. Because of that reputation, I was invited to contribute a chapter on career development to the second edition of *The Magazine*, which at the time was published by a subsidiary of *Folio:*, the leading publication for the magazine industry. Additional details about that program are included in Chapter 3 of this book, focusing on in-house training considerations.

An immediate challenge as VP/editorial was how to discuss performance issues with staff. The typical approach, equally frustrating for supervisor and subordinate, was management by adjectives. I talk more about this flawed practice later on. I believed a capable editorial manager, using a reasonable metric, must decide how long it should take a staff member to do any job. This covered routine work – writing product items or doing production – as well as researching and writing the most complex "roundup" feature.

Applying quantitative standards to qualitative work was hardly popular. Still, it was a hot topic back in the 1970s, and my Lone Ranger–like work in this area got the attention of several industry program chairpersons. Thus, I began a 15-year run of delivering editorial performance workshops at *Folio:* conferences. In 1984, I published in *Folio:* what was considered by some to be the first definitive position paper on performance evaluation standards. Later, two personnel management articles written for *Folio:* were included in the 1991 edition of *The Handbook of Magazine Publishing*. A revised version of one those articles—"Editors: Don't Trip Over Personnel Hurdles"—appears in this book.

The value of quantitative standards—or as some publishers characterized them, "editorial performance metrics"—may never be resolved. What top management must realize, of course, is that there is no convenient one-size-fits-all approach. Metrics must be tailored to individual magazines; without that, the goals that editors may be asked to achieve will often prove unrealistic.

With the rise of the Internet and online media, the topic of quantitative performance standards assumed an even greater importance. An answer to the question of "how long it takes to do anything" became more urgent than ever as editorial staffs were saddled with dual roles of producing print and online issues. The amount of work required for online editorial soared as email newsletters zoomed from weekly to daily circulation. Much of my work in the last decade has been in response to this trend, and is covered in this book.

While at Gralla, I developed a competitive analysis system

that took both qualitative and quantitative considerations into account. I'm sometimes asked why it is not enough to focus only on qualitative considerations aspects. The reason is that, unfortunately, many advertisers want an easy yardstick with which to demystify the evaluation of business magazines. If you can prove you are doing more than your competitors—whether in terms of your use of graphics, your attention to specific product categories, the amount of research you publish, or other measures—selling your publication is that much easier.

A full description of how to apply quantitative competitive analysis to features, news, graphics, at-show issues, and post-show issues is provided in my first book, *Get Serious About Competitive Editorial Analysis*. If you like this book, and are motivated to get ahead of your competitors, you'll find that it provides similar take-away value.

In the meantime, I invite you to continue your progress through this book, and hope you profit from the journey!

1

Use Data to Enhance
Editorial Performance

Selling editorial staffs on the value of quantitative performance standards was clearly an unwelcome idea many years ago when I addressed the topic in a workshop at an industry conference, the Folio: Show. The nerve of insisting that most editorial tasks could be assigned a specific number of hours to complete them was absolutely repulsive to my listeners. They were outraged—with the most violent objections coming from the editor of a crossword puzzle magazine.

In those days I was the editorial vice president of a multititle magazine publisher, Gralla Publications. In that role, I saw a need to rise above the traditional management-by-adjectives approach to editorial performance measurement. To be sure, qualitative accomplishment was worth its weight in gold. But most editorial managers rarely considered how much time a writer or editor required to achieve that level of excellence.

Happily, my own staff was graced with several editorial superstars willing to consider quantitative standards. They readily accepted job-description goals based on "how long it takes to do anything." The ability to deliver qualitative work in a quantitative way became a talking point I used when screening all job applicants.

Today, the rise of online media has only intensified the need for quantitative evaluation. Perhaps even more so than in print, quantitative yardsticks need to be developed and applied when measuring online editorial staff performance.

My first effort at creating a quantitative online performance model came via conducting a mini-study in preparation for a webinar sponsored by the American Society of Business Publication Editors (ASBPE). Later in this chapter, I will discuss key findings of that study.

But first, let's review how quantitative performance principles have been traditionally applied to print publications.

Establish realistic quantitative performance goals

Many editorial managers still believe quantitative standards cannot be applied to qualitative-oriented jobs. This, as some editors may have come to accept, is only partially true. In fact, qualitative and quantitative responsibilities can co-exist peacefully. Without quantitative guidelines, you lack a productive measurement required in order to define efficiency expectations.

To be an effective "qualitative person," you must know how long it realistically takes to complete any editorial assignment, from routine back-of-book departments to the most complex roundup features. This input makes it easier to create specific quantitative standards for routine tasks. For instance, how many product items can someone produce in a seven- or eight-hour day? How long should it take to turn out a batch of personnel appointment items or news briefs?

Let's look at some specific examples. Suppose an associate editor consistently delivers high-quality features. Does that mean that the process of feature writing is being executed in a superior way? Not necessarily, especially if the associate takes several weeks to develop a relatively simple article, and is consistently late with assignments.

The "slow but sure" person frequently burdens other staff members who must take on extra work that has been left undone. Perhaps that effect was manageable in the days of print-only work. But with the advent of online tasks, picking up slack becomes a more urgent responsibility.

In another scenario, say you have a copy editor on a products-only tabloid who is great in terms of quality. Is the work acceptable if he or she takes a half hour to edit each item? And how about the overzealous news department editor who takes four days to research a half-page article? Is it okay that half of the news section is late as a result?

On the other side of the coin, work habits are hardly the only cause of productivity slippage. In fact, digital workloads have been piled on existing staff with no relief offered in the form of additional staff. Then you have the situation where quantitative performance may be fine, but qualitative delivery is less than the best.

For all these reasons and more, you must develop reasonable, achievable quantitative standards covering all print and digital tasks. And the sooner you do so the better: if standards are in place when an editor first takes on a job, it's much easier than if you introduce them after a person has held the job for several years.

The process of creating these controls requires some agreement between editorial management and staff members as to how much time is required to perform basic tasks. Be forewarned, however, that in some cases staffers have difficulty thinking about their duties in terms of time.

Now, should you go all out and attach a time factor to every job component? Probably not. Instead, begin by assigning time factors to routine work that can be done more or less by rote in every issue.

The first step in search of better quantitative controls is to identify measurable components. For print, a typical starting point could include time spent on original writing, copyediting, production, travel, article recruitment, and administrative responsibilities.

Once you've arrived at quantitative yardsticks for, say, a monthly publication, conduct a "20-day test" assessment of every staff job. (If on-line job descriptions are being formulated, a five-day assessment may be more logical.) This means enumerating each task pertaining to that job, and then assigning a certain number of days or hours to complete everything within the average number of working hours per month. If the total number of days for a 20-day month is 25, you may have an overburdened editor on your hands.

In practice, quantitative standards allow a faster response to staff complaints that workloads are unreasonable.

Whenever editors express such concerns, invite them to run their own 20-day time-spent analysis of how their various tasks add up. If the self-analysis shows that the editors are working inefficiently, you can suggest time-saving short cuts.

Travel tracking requires special report

Quantitative analysis is not just useful for in-office activities. It can also pay dividends with editorial travel. Every field trip should produce editorial coverage that can be documented via staff-wide summaries. A well-constructed expense voucher should yield the necessary information in terms of time spent producing one or more articles.

The report I used to analyze editorial travel was compiled every six months. It showed total travel days for an entire magazine staff as well as average travel days per editor. The report included a similar calculation for the editor-in-chief. This was used to determine both that the top editor was living up to commitments to be in the field, but also that other staff members were being exposed to the field rather than being buried in the office.

Further, I compared what the data showed with the minimum travel guidelines for editorial staff. I expected top editors to be in the field at least three to five days a month, and junior editors to hit the road an average of two days per month.

There is another calculation you can derive from such data if you color-code your entries and translate the results into the percentage of time spent visiting readers at their places of business versus the percentage spent at trade shows. Finally, you need a table showing how the number of days in the field translates into number of pages or stories appearing in print or online.

If you really are gung-ho about travel tracking, you could also develop a "city-spread" analysis. By looking at the cities visited, you may discover that while an editorial staff may be racking up extensive travel, their effort is limited to a small number of major city destinations. In many industries, such a pattern may be unacceptable. Instead, for their industries, the boondocks are really where it's at in terms of satisfying a true cross-section of readers.

I will admit that my travel-tracking system is time-consuming. But the effort is worthwhile for anyone seeking the most accurate and useful editorial productivity analysis.

Digital work clearly time consuming

In the study I conducted for the ASBPE webinar, I surveyed 16 editors of business-to-business (B2B) magazines about their titles' online activities. The challenge to establish digital workload standards clearly was more complex than those posed by print. With print, analysis was based on seven fairly well-defined work categories. With digital, there were at least a dozen components worth considering.

After listing digital editing job components, the respondents answered a follow-up question designed to show the major time-eaters among online duties.

Topping the list was online news production, which could be subdivided into three categories: original writing, editing the work of others, and searching for story leads.

The second important time-eater was social media activity, which in some cases included blogging and monitoring discussion forums.

Other time-consuming activities included, in descending order of the time commitment required, posting or updating web content (which included coding and image processing), webinars and videos, and writing exclusive web-only features. Further down the list were website-analytics review, digital magazine contributions, and site redesign meetings.

The most accurate way to estimate online time components is by filling out a time sheet arranged in 15-minute brackets. Many editors say it's impossible to do that because the typical workload schedule involves jumping in and out of multiple activities all day long. If this is true, it's time for you to find ways to control schedule hyperactivity.

At the time I conducted this poll, most respondents estimated that they devoted 20 hours per week to online tasks. If they were to tabulate the actual time occupied by each of 12 or more tasks, however, their total time calculation might mushroom into something more like 25 or 30 hours.

Existing time allotted to digital editorial activities may be sufficient to allow editors to meet quantitative deadlines. But meeting qualitative standards is another matter, especially when it comes to online news writing. Many industry observers think judgments about content excellence will be influenced by evidence of enterprise and exclusivity. Within the time frame available to you and your staff, how well do you deliver on these requirements compared to your toughest competitors? What would it take in terms of time for you to be assured of bragging rights in head-to-head comparisons?

Specific time estimates provided by survey respondents indicate the productivity challenge involved. For instance, one editor-in-chief devotes 10 hours a week to social media and discussion forums. Another editor-in-chief spends seven hours a week on social media, 75 percent of which is focused on marketing posts. An executive editor spends 10 hours a week tracking down, editing, and writing online news stories. Another five to seven hours is devoted to production, including resizing and editing images as well as HTML coding.

Online workload challenges

Candid comments gathered from the survey reflected the burden that resulted when management dumped additional workloads on staffs already strapped by print magazine responsibilities. In addition, several complaints lamented time devoted to marketing department projects that should have died a quicker death. A few of those responses follow. Undoubtedly, most of these comments will have a familiar ring to current B2B editors.

"Ad revenue is nonexistent for the digital products we have going on already, much less the new ones we've been asked to develop. I've voiced my fear we're doing too much, and I've been told that our page views are outstanding, so we should simply keep going, because it's paying off. Meanwhile, my sanity and the sanity of our one other editor is quickly slipping away." —*Editor-in-chief*

"Digital workload definitely can become inflated when publishers are trying to push too many projects for too long a trial period. Our editors don't spend time on stuff that is supposed to generate advertising but doesn't work. Our major concern is giving readers what they want as opposed to forcing content down their throats." —*President/group editorial director*

"We probably are producing 20 percent more content, so something has to slide. I don't have time to do big picture stuff. Our editors are still traveling, but not as many people as in the past are budgeted to cover industry events." *—Editor-in-chief*

"We don't have the people, time or technology to handle more projects (like webinars). When the technology becomes available, I expect to be asked to take on more projects. At one point, digital editions were carbon copies of the regular print issue. But now we are being asked to create original copy for digital issues." *—Executive editor*

"Our average workload per week is up from 45-50 hours to 60 hours. Work activity doesn't stop when you leave the office. At night I will check my e-mails on my phone and then answer messages requiring priority response." *—Editor-in-chief*

Online work has advantages

Not all survey responses conveyed resentment of online responsibilities:

"One real benefit we've seen from the on-line workload involves trade show coverage. We make it a priority to write up news immediately after events and get it on-line ASAP. This not only means we have the most current content, but when we return from the show, our work (at least as far as press event coverage goes) is essentially done. Our sales staff makes a point of sending the links to this 'from-the-show' coverage to our advertisers." *—Senior VP, editorial*

"Web involvement has allowed me to build my own brand by engaging in social media discussions. The investment in time has clearly paid off. Editorial peers are not eager to follow suit because of time involvement. My perspective is that social media should be used for conversation and relationship building purposes, not so much for pushing out promotional messages. The number of sources to be monitored has grown tremendously. When our industry was smaller, there were perhaps 20 sites that needed to be checked out. Today, I have feeds from 270 blogs and try to get to all of them every day." — *Editor-in-chief*

As these comments from my survey indicate, the workload requirements imposed by online activities are creating significant stresses on editorial staffs. If you've yet to conduct your own productivity analysis, don't delay further. Your future workload is only likely to increase. You must be able to handle the added quantitative challenge in a qualitative way.

2

Twelve Common Management Errors

E ditorial personnel management is probably the most important responsibility falling within the editor-in-chief's job description. With the arrival of online media, it has become even more important, but at the same time, even more elusive. In today's hectic editorial environment, editorial managers may be strongly tempted to ignore the basic best practices of staff supervision and motivation.

Compounding this problem is the fact that many of today's B2B editorial managers have not been groomed for a supervisory role. Yet dealing with staff probably occupies most of their time and causes them the most grief. If all we had to do was create great editorial material, design terrific magazines, devise an effective marketing strategy in cooperation with a publisher or sales manager, and not need to worry about how other people did their jobs, our lives would be easier.

In an effort to clarify personnel management challenges, I devised a workshop that addressed 12 common mistakes that editorial managers make and suggested ways to overcome them. Let's take a closer look at each mistake:

1. Neglecting to pre-screen a seemingly experienced editor's basic skills.

Insisting on a skills test in the hiring process is not an indictment of experienced writers. Unfortunately, an applicant's clippings are not always an indicator of writing skill. There may have been heavy editing of the applicant's work, on a consistent basis, by another party. If that's the case, you need to know beforehand—but the applicant may not be inclined to confess. You'll feel better about making the hire if the applicant passes your screening process with flying colors, which is exactly what should happen.

Consider the down side. You decide not to test the applicant's writing skills—and suddenly you find that you have acquired a lemon. Your content suffers. Worse, junior staff members are quick to notice when an experienced newcomer who joined the staff at a much higher salary level just doesn't have it. Now you also have a morale problem on your hands.

So why take a chance? Instead, ensure that every editorial staff candidate completes some form of written test unless you can personally vouch for the candidate's ability.

2. Prolonging the hiring process.

This mistake is most likely to haunt you when you are considering hiring a recent, talented college graduate. If your hiring process takes a few days because there are many interviews and a test in the bargain, you may lose a promising candidate to a competitor who takes one look and says, "You're hired."

Outstanding editorial candidates are scarce these days. Therefore, it is to your advantage to complete your entire screening process in a single day. Of course, a written test requirement is not the only reason the hiring process gets stalled. It can be difficult to schedule time for all the interviewers. The more members you have on your screening committee, the harder it will be to streamline the selection process.

3. Failing to document poor performance.

Many supervising editors still prefer to rely on verbal feedback as a way to cure an errant staff member. Don't fall into this trap! Wiser managers have learned—usually the hard way—that written records are essential to staff improvement and oversight.

This means you must convince a problem staff member that you are carefully documenting performance shortfalls in meeting deadlines and productivity levels as well as recording lateness and absence patterns.

If you consistently rewrite an editor's work, that editor should be furnished with "before" and "after" versions of each manuscript. An accompanying memo should spell out why the changes were made.

4. Deferring confrontations.

Let's say that you have been keeping careful written records and find, unhappily, that you have a case for correction. When will you bring the matter to a head? Unfortunately, the annual salary review often is the first time that a staff member learns of a superior's dissatisfaction. What's even worse is when the staffer is not hearing this directly from the boss, but from the human resources personnel.

Effective criticism must be scheduled closely on the heels of the infraction – not several weeks or months later, when the next official performance review is scheduled.

5. Failing to forestall premature burnout.

Because there is a certain amount of routine work associated with most editorial positions, burnout can occur at any of the various stages of an editorial career. It all depends on how long it takes those routine aspects to eliminate the excitement once associated with the job. Editors-in-chief are just as subject to burnout as subordinates. Clearly it's harder for a bored boss to pump up sagging staff spirits. But assuming that editorial management is highly motivated, much can be done to forestall burnout of subordinates.

A key practice is to keep routine tasks under control. Share such work among all staff members—don't dump it all on an editorial assistant or assistant editor. Routine definitely sinks junior editors first. If they joined your staff because you led them to believe there would be creative assignments attached to the job, but all they do is proofread pages and write back-of-book material, they'll soon be history.

Senior editors grow restless because, at some point, covering the same industry day after day becomes tedious. Top management must anticipate this problem by varying responsibilities. It's even a good idea to delegate plum assignments as often as possible.

Finally, accept the fact that some staff members will just get tired of being editors. For them, writing has become a chore. Attending conventions is torture. Field trips interfere with personal obligations more often. Sometimes the only solution in such cases is an amicable separation.

6. Writing abusive communications to subordinates.

You believe in documenting faulty performance, but sometimes you let your emotions take control when communicating with an errant staff member. True, you feel great after completing the memo detailing the staffer's failures (after all, you got off a few splendid barbs). But now that you have vented, treat your initial effort as a first draft. Delete all the subjectivity and create a document worthy of an objective manager. Memos with nasty overtones can come back to haunt you, even if you are the editor-in-chief.

7. Overlooking the anti-writing syndrome.

Most journalists choose their careers because they love to write. But years later, some of them fall victim to what I call the "anti-writing syndrome." That is, they discover that writing has become what they least like to do.

When your best editors no longer write, the quality of the content suffers. In too many cases, the only written contribution by the editor-in-chief—typically the most experienced and knowledgeable staffer—is a short editorial column. All too often, the result is key assignments being given to junior staffers, who produce articles that are far from authoritative. In such situations, there is an urgent need for editorial management to jump into the writing pit.

A better approach, of course, is for the editor-in-chief to set an example for staff from the outset, regularly contributing outstanding coverage of some critical facet of the industry covered. The editor-in-chief's level of reporting reflects a background and intuition that no other staff member can provide.

8. Ignoring the procrastinator/perfectionist pattern.

You have a writer whose work always is magnificent when completed. Unfortunately, it seems to take this person longer than anyone else to finish any assignment. Do you overlook weaknesses because of the strengths? It's much easier to do so if you have a very large staff. But it may prove catastrophic if you have only two or three staff editors to turn out a magazine with a substantial content requirement.

The procrastinator/perfectionist is not easily spotted during the screening process. The best defense you have is a set of quantitative standards before you begin hiring. Articulate these standards when screening all editorial applicants, repeat the discussion during each new editor's orientation, and support all this with written job descriptions that include quantitative expectations.

9. Allowing chain-of-command by-passers.

Inevitably, you may have to deal with a subordinate who refuses to accept direction from anyone other than the editor-in-chief. This chain-of-command by-passer argues with the managing editor over every manuscript change. Somehow every disagreement this individual has makes its way into the editor-in-chief's office.

If as the supervisor you allow this to happen, you are guilty of undermining your subordinate management team. Yes, all staff members should have contact with the top editorial gun, but under clearly defined ground rules. Some publishers include a "reporting responsibility" paragraph in all job descriptions as a useful means of underscoring the proper chain of command.

10. Not addressing the editorial inferiority complex. This may be one of the biggest errors many editorial managers make. Here I am referring to an attitude sometimes assumed by staff editors to the effect of, "salespeople are important, we aren't." Sometimes editors have this attitude because they reject the idea that publishing should be run in a business-like way. But more often it reflects a broader cultural problem within the company as a whole. How do you handle this, especially when business is really tough?

Ultimately, the solution to this problem must come from the publisher. Astute publishers make it a point to commend the editorial staff for outstanding feature material, as opposed to carping endlessly about an advertiser who was omitted from a roundup story or complaining that the opposition runs more back-of-the-book material, especially personnel announcements. In addition, some publishers hold training seminars just for editors. This can offset the feeling that training efforts are directed at salespeople only.

11. Viewing training as an inconvenience. At one time early in your career, you may have gotten a big kick out of training junior editors. But once you began experiencing turnover—as so often happens at that level—the ongoing need to retrain new editors took the fun out of being a teacher. Now you may find yourself following in the footsteps of other hard-pressed chief editors, who delegated the training job to a subordinate or simply halted all training activity.

If the delegate is a competent trainer, you're okay. On the

other hand, it's still your responsibility to make sure that the lessons being taught are the lessons you want learned. Training is an extremely important function. You must stay involved in that process in one way or another if you are interested in perpetuating a strong bench of capable, up-and-coming staff editors.

12. Filling the empty stall in a panic.
An assistant editor just resigned, and there isn't a replacement in sight. Three people have to do the work of four until somebody runs an ad or calls an employment agency, interviews candidates, and makes a decision.

In a situation like this, when you have an empty stable, there is a tendency to hire in a hurry. A happier alternative is to anticipate the need to hire, making an ongoing effort to screen promising candidates, even when there is no job opening. Better yet, if you are in the rare position of having a budget that can handle it, hire a promising entry-level applicant as a trainee. Then, the next time you have a sudden departure, you'll have a promising replacement ready.

3

Commit to In-House Training

Y ou will have noticed that nearly all of the 12 management hurdles outlined in the previous chapter directly involve hiring, training, or review of editorial staff. If these hurdles taken together strike you as overwhelming, you are not alone.

In this chapter, we'll look at how to create a foundation for effective and efficient approaches to hiring and training editorial staff.

Make an all-out effort

Many B2B publishers give lip service to the importance of editorial excellence. But when they are asked to describe the extent of the support they provide to achieve it, training—especially in-house training—is lacking. This is not acceptable. Instead, an all-out effort is mandatory.

Exactly how do I define "all out"? The best answer I can offer is to describe the training program in place during my experience at Gralla Publications. Some years ago, I provided details on the program in an interview included in *The Magazine*, a worthy career guide published by Folio's book division. If that division still existed today, I would recommend that you buy this valuable guide.

Instead, you will have to settle for a summary of the Q&A interview. There is a lot to compare with whatever your entry-level development plan is now.

Many Gralla practices of yesteryear deserve imitation today. Gralla was one of the few major trade publishing companies to maintain a formal training program for candidates fresh out of school. Our program combined job rotation, a series of workshops, and "second opinions" on all feature articles written while a trainee. Each trainee received a 10-week agenda that involved assignments on four or five of our magazines. Our training program coordinator scheduled additional 10-week schedules for the trainee until he or she moved onto one magazine as an assistant editor. (For more on this approach to rotating trainees through various magazines, see "Consider a Floater Program" on page 29.)

Workshops took place monthly during regular office hours and ran as long as two hours. Topics included how to cover a trade show, math facts for editors, common editorial goofs (my favorite), interviewing techniques, story sources, headline and lede writing, graphics for tabloids, graphics for standard size magazines, editorial performance management, and understanding production. The workshops were highly interactive and included challenging exercises. When applicable, a homework assignment was part of the course. The following workshop summaries reflect the typical content.

Magazine launch strategy. In this session, the leader would present a scenario describing an upcoming magazine debut. Participants were asked to devise an editorial plan that included advance research of competitive magazines, choice of standard-size or tabloid format, editorial page count, and number of full-time staff members. The attendees had half an hour to devise a plan, after which all proposals were reviewed.

Hit Parade of Editorial Goofs. This company-wide workshop was usually held at least once a year. Participants completed several five-minute editing exercises based on the most common errors found in their publications. When presenting this session, I would reserve the final 15 minutes for an exercise devoted to "18 Spectacular Editing Goofs." While challenging, the session also was fun, particularly as attendees groaned when they learned how many mistakes they had missed.

A program of this scope is most easily achieved by larger publishers. However, for editors at smaller companies who have only one or two staff members, a modified program is within reach. The trainer, presumably the editor-in-chief, must set aside an hour a day during the first 10 days of a newcomer's employment for that purpose. For a sample hour-a-day schedule, continue reading!

Practice systematic on-board training

There is perhaps no more important time for training staff than when they first come on board. I recommend three ways to interact with entry-level staff members:

1. First day orientation.
Set aside 60 to 90 minutes for this meeting, during which the following agenda might be covered:

- Productivity standards
- Organization techniques
- Writing tips
- Submitting travel expenses
- The use of e-mail and other written communications
- The need to obtain full instructions on all assignments
- Photography technique
- Tracking competitive publications/on-line media
- Redress/appeal procedures.

2. Periodic "read list" reviews.
At Gralla, I saw a need for a policy that allowed tracking the performance of entry-level staff assigned to various magazines. My solution was organizing a "read list" agenda. This required all new editors to give me copies of every manu-

script assigned by any immediate superior that they felt was ready for submission. My job was to provide feedback for a period of up to six months. In this way, new staffers were guaranteed feedback. At the same time, I could confirm that their supervisors were providing creative assignments.

3. Hour-a-day training.

With new editors fresh out of college, starting them off on the right foot is critical. The hour-a-day approach recommended here works with the smallest of staffs. I employed it myself whenever supervising a B2B magazine that only allowed for two editors—the editor-in-chief and an assistant. The premise is that for two consecutive weeks—or the 10 consecutive days that the training editor is in the office—one hour a day is mandated for "classroom work" with the new recruit.

Of course, you can take this effort beyond 10 days. No matter what the eventual schedule, the one required ingredient is commitment. Many editors, especially those with very small staffs and very big workloads, believe training is out of the question. This attitude is unfortunate. It leads to new editors losing interest very quickly in their job and diminishing their career potential.

The ten-day schedule I used most of the time, shown below, is evenly split between basics and industry background. It presumes that new recruits also are required to spend at least another hour a day reading back issues of the magazine, making notes, and then raising questions during the regular training sessions.

Day 1. General orientation. Magazine philosophy and position. Career potential. Importance of being an industry authority. Complaint-handling policy.

Day 2. Editorial objectives. Style requirements. Graphics. How production schedule works.

Day 3. Editing principles. Headline and caption writing. Importance of tightly written copy and how to achieve it. How to create exciting leads. Story organization. (This class is illustrated with frequent references to strengths and weaknesses of recent issues of the magazine or website in question.)

Day 4. Interviewing techniques and story development. Information sources. Critical questions to ask during most interviews. How and when to write a query letter. How to qualify prospective interviewees.

Day 5. Trade show coverage techniques. Advance planning. Photography ideas. Seeking editorial exclusivity. Sales-editorial teamwork.

Day 6. Industry background. History. Terminology. Distribution structure. Market data.

Day 7. Industry background (continued). Key industry issues – past, present, future.

Day 8. Magazine's position in the marketplace vs. competition. Strengths and weaknesses.

Day 9. Key industry associations. History of our magazine's relationship with major groups. Review of important industry conventions.

Day 10. Role of other departments: Sales. Promotion. Circulation. Accounting. Production.

The above sequence can of course be modified to suit your magazine or website. And if you can devote even more time than an hour a day to training during the early stages, so much the better.

The larger your company and the more top management supports training activity, the more you can expand upon this basic training outline. Beware complacency or the temptation to skip personal involvement in a new recruit's training. Do not forfeit this valuable opportunity!

Consider a floater training program

The practice of rotating new entry-level editors through several publications, or "floater" training programs, works well for multi-title publishers with at least five or six publications in the shop. But even small enterprises may be able to adapt this system.

The floater is an entry-level assistant editor who has demonstrated superstar potential during the job-screening process. In practice, the floater receives a ten-week schedule that provides experience working on three or four publications or websites. If a full-time opening has not materialized during the initial 10 weeks, the schedule is renewed until a full-time, regular staff position is available. During this period, the floater has limited exposure to other departments such as circulation and production.

At Gralla, many editors who began as floaters rose to management positions within three years. At its peak, the program included four floaters at the same time. A standing requirement for editors who requested floater assistance was that their entry-level assistants would be given creative assignments. Supervising editors also were expected to submit performance reviews covering their assigned floater's management potential.

At many publishing companies, entry-level editors who are immediately placed on one title end up buried in drudgery.

They become a dumping ground for tedious work that other staff members are eager to pawn off on someone else. What a waste of talent! And of course, it's a reason why at some firms, entry-level posts become a revolving door. A well-managed floater program can avoid this problem.

Create self-scoring profiles

An excellent way to encourage interactivity during an in-house workshop is to have participants work their way through selected self-scoring editorial quizzes, or profiles. Creating these instructive profiles requires trainers to think through the scheduled topic to come up with 10 to 15 factors for self-assessment. As the class begins, the profile is distributed to the class. After all of the factors are explained, the attendees score their performance in terms of how well they execute each factor.

While profiles can be created for virtually any topic, there are five in particular that I use regularly:

- Becoming someone in your industry
- Complaint handling
- Feature writing
- Editorial marketing arsenal (see Chapter 6)
- Trade show coverage (see Chapter 9)

BECOMING SOMEONE IN YOUR INDUSTRY SELF-SCORING PROFILE

Entry-level editors eventually can become recognized industry authorities given proper guidance. The key vehicle for getting there sooner rather than later is visibility. Consistently writing important feature articles is imperative. But equally important, if not more so, is becoming a known personality. This is more likely to occur when staff members travel frequently. The self-scoring profile on the next page suggests ways of "becoming someone" worth considering.

Action	Score
I make field trips constantly.	
I write a feature article in every issue.	
I am conversant with every new industry trend.	
I would have no problem writing a research article.	
I generate a constant stream of correspondence.	
I have no problem making a speech.	
I get involved in association activities.	
I suggest publicity angles constantly.	
I wield a mighty tennis racket and/or golf club.	
I regularly attend convention hospitality events.	
I know my reporting is 100 percent accurate.	
I regularly exchange business cards at industry functions.	
I keep abreast of other department activities.	
I read my competition regularly.	
I look like "someone" when I go into the field.	
Total Score:	
Scoring key: Total score for 15 factors = 100 points. Assign 1 to 10 points per factor depending upon how you value performance. The usual guideline is that five factors can earn maximum of 10 points; remaining factors can earn maximum of five points.	

COMPLAINT-HANDLING SELF SCORING PROFILE

Successful handling of complaints involves two related categories of actions: responses made to a complaint and the policies to anticipate and reduce complaints. When you pay sufficient attention to the second category, of course, instances of the first category will decrease. The profile on the next page assesses both categories.

Action	Score
I respond to all complaints within 24 hours.	
When a complaint is received by phone, I take careful notes and read them back to the complaining party. Then I inquire if any other problem exists.	
I inform top management of all complaints immediately.	
I always obtain all available legal documentation before writing about lawsuits and related matters.	
I make sure all advertorial copy is identified as such.	
I delete unsubstantiated claims of superiority buried in new product releases.	
I obtain vendor okay before excerpting content from their websites.	
If interviewing vendors for roundup articles, I keep accurate records of attempts to reach parties who subsequently claim they were overlooked in published articles quoting their competitors.	
During the initial response to a complaint, I give a deadline by which a resolution will be reached; I always abide by that deadline.	
When working with freelance writers, I take special care to review payment policies; I always advise the freelancer in writing about payment for a specific assignment and the absolute deadline for receipt of the assignment.	
Total Score:	

Scoring key: Assign 1 to 10 points per action depending upon how you rate your performance. The total maximum score is 100 points. The above profile includes four actions falling into category 1; six reflect category 2 anticipatory actions.

FEATURE WRITING SELF-SCORING PROFILE

This is the most basic among my five favorite profiles. It addresses 15 factors that usually come into play in writing feature articles.

Action	Score
First three paragraphs of article are loaded with facts of importance to all readers.	
Lede offers a preview of all key story points.	
Lede emphasizes what's new, not what's history.	
Sidebars are provided for all long features.	
All persons quoted are fully identified.	
Everything in the article makes sense to the author.	
Examples are used to tailor "general" articles.	
Decks supplement rather than echo headlines.	
Captions are story-telling as opposed to just performing label function.	
Most paragraphs and sentences are kept short.	
"Profile" articles attempt to focus on a limited number of themes.	
Feature writing format varies.	
Examples containing numbers/quantitative results are cited often.	
Graphic needs are considered during story development phase.	
Survey reports interpret rather than just cite facts.	
Total Score:	

Scoring key: Total maximum score equals 100 points. Each factor can earn maximum score of five or 10 points depending on your current editing policy. In practice, five priority factors earn 10 points; the remaining factors earn five points.

BONUS PROFILE: THE EDITORIAL MIRACLE WORKER

One profile I use at conference presentations is designed to identify what I call Editorial Miracle Workers. The realization that editors must wear many hats beyond the traditional ones started to spread in the late 1990s. At that time, the trend was for management to urge editors to play a stronger marketing role.

The situation prompted me to create and introduce my first multi-hat profile at a Folio conference. I listed 10 diversified roles editors were being challenged to play: magician, assassin, marketing wizard, technology expert, graphics guru, show business star, teacher, industry maven-statistician, customer service specialist, and highly skilled editor-writer.

Today, especially in view of increasing online involvement, the list of roles editors are asked to play has clearly expanded. But the key question remains the same: Are editors willing and prepared to play each role to the hilt?

For each role described in this two-part profile, ask the editors to rate their ability. The maximum score possible is 100 points. If their final score falls below 80, ask them to consider how factors inhibiting their performance can be improved.

Part I: For each of the 10 roles below, rate your performance on a 1 to 7 point scale, 7 being best.	
Magician: Constantly delivers top-quality content, even though frequently saddled by a restricted budget.	
Assassin: Candidly assesses editorial strength and weakness versus the competition, then provides evaluation results to the marketing group.	
Marketing Wizard: Periodically recommends projects/supplements that offer solid ad potential for marketing purposes.	
Technology Expert: Rarely baffled by computer and website glitches.	
Graphics Guru: Conjures up snazzy layout ideas. Also battles proposed designs that are esthetically interesting but less than reader friendly.	
Show Business Pro: Always a star performer before audiences and constantly in demand as a speaker.	
Teacher: Personally involved in training and providing feedback to staff members. Embraces reality of training as a never-ending task.	
Industry Maven/Statistician: Data-adept in terms of creating, interpreting, and publishing surveys that address groundbreaking issues.	
Customer Service Specialist: Adheres to a written policy describing optional ways to resolve editorial complaints.	
Visible Editorial Contributor: This role is especially critical for editors-in-chief. If their contribution per issue rarely goes beyond an editorial column, they are falling short. Maximum score is possible only for the editorial manager who consistently by-lines timely features.	

Part II: For each of the two roles below, rate yourself on a 1 to 15 point scale, 15 being best.	
Webmaster: Maintains a timely, fast-paced, easily navigated site. Capably channels readers back and forth among e-newsletters, websites, and publications. Constantly delivers exclusive website material. Evaluates strengths and weaknesses versus competitors. Somehow capably executes this role while fulfilling all other responsibilities in exemplary manner.	
Management Problem Solver: Website involvement has heightened the importance of this role. Frequently, without benefit of any "upsizing," the editors regularly update sites, generate one or more e-newsletters, and simultaneously deliver a four-star publication. This accomplishment is indeed a miracle.	
Total Score:	

4

Quantitative Factors Improve Staff Reviews

C an editorial jobs, highly qualitative in nature, be evaluated quantitatively for performance review purposes? The quick answer is "yes." If you're not accustomed to using numbers as part of your personnel reviews, don't worry. Once a few preliminary steps are taken, an effective blending of qualitative and quantitative standards is within reach.

The first step towards more accurate performance reviews, of course, is to establish estimates of how long it should take to complete typical editorial tasks. For the purpose of this discussion, let's assume you've already done that. Next, update existing job descriptions to include quantitative performance expectations. Finally, you probably need to create a performance review form that links those expectations with appropriate descriptions of qualitative requirements.

Are you ready to give this approach a shot in the interests of achieving a higher degree of performance review accuracy? If so, read on.

Avoid management by adjectives

A major hurdle early in my B2B editorial career was contending with so-called constructive criticism from supervisors. In many cases, the interaction was a management-by-adjectives affair. Yes, the need for improvement on my part was necessary. But the direction I received often left me in a guessing game.

Assessments of questionable value included comments such as, "you took too long to write that article," "your work needs tightening," or "you aren't writing enough new product items a day." Sometimes I was blessed with that most unhelpful recommendation of all, "your introduction isn't crisp enough."

Faced with this vague feedback, I vowed that if I ever got to be an editorial manager, I would quantify performance as much as possible. Over the following years, that's exactly what I did.

Whether or not you wish to include quantitative requirements in job descriptions depends upon the need to pin down specific staff members to stipulated workloads. For example, let's say a job description for an assistant editor of a promotion/marketing tabloid specifies a monthly responsibility of writing the up-front news section. This encompasses six to eight long articles plus a few shorts, all of this averaging a total of 150 to 200 inches per month (or 5 to 6.5 full pages in standard-size magazine format). In addition, the assistant furnishes photo captions and news briefs about current promotions, amounting to 50 inches per month.

Another assistant editor's job description—this one involving a retail publication—notes that the role involves all new products, literature, and merchandising sections. This entails writing from 40 to 200 product items each month, depending on size of issue. There will be a minimum of 20 literature items monthly.

The quantitative job description definitely is a good place for an editorial manager to state how much time routine tasks should occupy. How long does it really take to write a product section? Or some of the other back-of-book departments? Or to update the calendar?

You can get into quantitative evaluation of feature writing at a later date. In the meantime, analyzing detail work will result in a good indication of the benefit to you of having a firmer handle on the time required to complete different types of projects.

Tailor your performance review form

Once quantitative job descriptions are in place, it's time to create a tailored editorial performance evaluation form. Your key objective here is to define qualitative expectations for various job levels.

At some publishing companies, editorial staffs contend with corporate formats that don't come close to pinpointing specific strengths and weaknesses. In contrast, other firms have produced tailored forms that lend themselves to a more precise appraisal.

Some of those forms are quite elaborate. They include standard rating systems ("on the basis of one to five, rate staff member's copy editing ability"). Other forms become more complex, assigning quantitative values to the effective execution of specific job functions. Indeed, some evaluation forms are needlessly heavy on detail.

Now let's look at a performance review form one company uses to assess five editorial management factors. The system involves scoring of one to five points, with one being the best. Here's how scoring criteria are defined:

1 = consistently exceeds requirements of job.

2 = often exceeds requirements of job.

3 = meets basic requirements of job.

4 = does not always meet requirements of job; needs remedial effort.

5 = marked failure to meet requirements of job.

(If it were my company, I would reverse scoring definitions so as to make five indicate the best performance rather than worst.)

In the excerpt that follows, the series of questions are addressed to the person completing the evaluation form, who in theory supervises the editorial manager being reviewed.

1. How would you rate this individual's news judgment? Consider ability to judge value and importance of a story; proficiency in detecting story inadequacies; ability to detect libel; ability to properly judge length; ability to weigh merits of completing stories and stories from different sources on same subject; and ability to communicate with others on major changes in stories.

2. How would you rate this individual's ability to assign stories? Consider ability to originate stories; ability to foresee problems in reporting and writing; and ability to match reporters with assignments.

3. How would you rate this individual's potential for supervision and leadership? Consider initiative, ability, or potential to develop, teach, and motivate subordinates; ability to reach compromises and otherwise solve problems; ability to coordinate with other desks; ability to delegate; and relationships with peers, subordinates, and supervisors.

4. How would you rate this individual's language skills? Consider ability to recognize dull or hackneyed prose and convert it to bright, original writing; ability to recognize work that does not require substantive changes; ability to eliminate the ambiguous, the wordy and the ungrammatical; and ability to write headlines and rewrite.

5. How would you rate this individual's ability to work under pressure? Consider ability to remake the paper or recast a story headline or a page for a breaking development near deadline; and ability to meet deadlines.

For each of the five factors the form provides comment areas in which the reviewer can indicate where the editor requires improvement or is especially outstanding. There is additional space for summarizing the individual's strengths and weaknesses as a manager. Finally, there is a section in the form devoted to focusing on goals for the coming year.

If this format appeals to you, one of your questions could pertain to field presence. Something like:

How would you rate this individual's ability to represent your magazine in the field? Consider impression by appearance; whether or not the individual is articulate; grasp of current business trends in various fields; ability to make friends easily; skills at preparing innovative A/V presentations; and ability to work well with advertisers.

If a scoring range of 1 to 5 seems too limited, you could use 1 to 10. Personally, I think a 10-point system is needlessly complicated. But here's how one publishing company did it:

1 = unsatisfactory—requires immediate improvement.
2 = satisfactory—acceptable performance but improvement needed.
3 = satisfactory—acceptable performance but improvement desirable.
4 = satisfactory—acceptable performance and showing improvement.
5 = good—no serious problems.
6 = good—always meets expectations.
7 = good—sometimes excellent.
8 = excellent—consistent, high-quality performance.

9 = superior—an example for others.
10 = outstanding—unquestionably the best.

The evaluation then scores eight areas:

- Knowledge/technical competence
- Original contribution
- Quality of writing and presentation
- Planning, scheduling, and organization
- Field work
- Teamwork
- Effort
- General skills

When reviewing a senior editor in knowledge and technical competence, the following attributes are scored:

> Keeps up on state of the art in assigned areas; grasps new developments in assigned areas; exercises good judgment in assessing what is technically important; keeps informed on industry technology in general.

For original contribution, these attributes are weighed:

> Writes articles appropriately for assigned coverage; proposes articles for improved coverage; contributes to development of effective cover; anticipates readers' information needs; participates in editorial meetings and discussions; contributes ideas for improvement of magazines in general.

For fieldwork, the following considerations apply:

> Keeps in touch with companies and experts in editor's area of specialization; develops sources and contacts for articles and information; participates in appropriate organizations; attends appropriate meetings, seminars, and conventions;

maintains good liaison with public relations people and others.

Based on the preceding examples, you can see that tailored evaluation forms also have potential for copy editors, artists, managing editors, photo editors, fact checkers, etc. For copy editors, a scoring range from 1 to 5 could rate performance in terms of the following attributes:

* Edits accurately, enforcing rules of grammar, usage, and house style
* Edits at the optimal speed for the type of content
* Consistently raises valid questions about story substance in addition to correcting grammar and spelling
* Adept at writing headlines and captions when required
* Interacts effectively with art department in resolving layout problems

For managing editors, a scoring range from 1 to 5 could be used to evaluate performance in terms of these attributes:

* Always ensures magazine is out on time
* Is excellent trainer
* Adept at writing headlines and captions
* Requires little supervision to reliably execute major projects
* Consistently gives valuable story-direction input to writers
* Has outstanding field presence
* Enjoys excellent relationship with superiors
* Offers clear potential become an editor-in-chief

Last but not least, as far as evaluation forms are concerned, one size definitely does not fit all. Attempts to make all evaluation forms the same will ultimately fail.

So if the tailored concept interests you, start slow. A logical place to embark would be with a description and evaluation form for an entry-level position. Your task will be easier, of course, if you already have quantitative performance standards in place!

5

Fourteen Causes of Editorial Burnout

The reasons for editorial career burnout vary, depending on whether the depressed staffer is junior or senior level. The most difficult management dilemmas involve senior staff. Burnout at this level is hastened by a build-up of job pressures that are traditionally part of the grind but are no longer easily tolerated. The burnout victims may be asking themselves a host of typical questions:

- Why do salespeople and account executives make more money than editors?
- Who needs all this deadline pressure?
- How can I handle all these increasing online responsibilities?
- How does top brass expect me to function with inexperienced junior editors?
- Why is management insensitive to editorial quality or the need for added editorial support?

To identify and address the symptoms of burnout, I have developed an editorial burnout scorecard. It considers 14 job components that are a regular part of a B2B editor's routine, or should be. As you consider them, ask yourself how many of these do you still find rewarding? And, if many of them have become a drag, how can you change things for the better?

In the scorecard on the next two pages, each of the burnout factors is assigned a scoring key specific to the type of factor in question. The score for each factor reflects the editor's level of satisfaction with that element of the job.

Burnout Factor	Score
I write at least one important feature every month. (Every issue = 5 points; occasionally = 2–5; rarely = 1; never = 0)	
If I write an editorial column, it is well thought out and timely, rather than hurriedly written at the last minute to fill the space. (Regular, thoughtful editorial = 5 points; occasional original thinking = 2–4; always pressing panic buttons = 1)	
I spend at least three days each month in the field meeting readers. (Always = 5 points; occasionally = 2–4; rarely = 1; never = 0)	
I reach out to new sources each month rather than rely on "old friends" as contacts. (Yes = 5 points; sometimes = 2–4; rarely = 0)	
I take personal interest in developing the skills of inexperienced staff members. (Allow 10 points if you regard yourself to be an outstanding teacher; otherwise = 1–9)	
I have developed written, flexible job descriptions for staff members. (Allow up to 5 points)	
When required, I furnish written job objectives that an errant staff member must meet within a specified time period. (Allow up to 10 points, depending on how consistently you follow this policy and on the degree to which you take action if no improvement is made.)	
I support an editorial chain of command that requires staff to resolve problems with immediate superiors before going to the editor-in-chief. (Allow up to 3 points)	

I introduce at least six new, exciting, timely features every year. (Allow up to 10 points)	
I land a speaking appearance on at least three or four industry programs every year. (Allow up to 4 points)	
I spend company money and administer corporate policies as if they were my own. (Allow up to 3 points)	
I consistently evaluate competitive magazines for strengths and weaknesses. (Allow up to 5 points)	
I read my own magazine promptly upon publication for goofs that our editing process overlooked. (Conduct postmortems for every issue = 5 points; never conduct postmortems = 0; occasional post-mortems = 1–4.)	
I meet all publication deadlines and expect the same of all staff members. (Allow up to 5 points)	
Total Score:	

If your overall enthusiasm hasn't dissolved in terms of executing the previous 14 factors, a top score of 80 points is possible. Start worrying if this exercise results in a number of zero scores.

Four more burnout signals

Besides the above 14 burnout factors, there are four signals related to an editor's state-of-mind. If any of these apply to you, your personal editorial burnout may be imminent.

- I am willing to accept second-best editorial material because of time constraints or staff weakness.
- I have paid my dues, so I don't have to pitch in to help the staff produce an issue.

- I don't like to travel anymore. I'll only go to trade shows where my attendance is mandatory. Otherwise I delegate these trips to staff.
- I believe there should be no provision for advertiser-related editorial in my magazine or on my website. I also don't believe I should be responsive to advertiser complaints.

Occasionally I include these four factors in other self-scoring profiles I use, in which case they would be scored negatively. For now, let's not concern ourselves with possible calculations. Instead, let's more carefully consider the circumstances that may bring each mindset to a head.

For instance, settling for second best arises when editors become less inclined to manage a staff, especially when dealing with laggard performers. Delaying the inevitable is a bad idea and reduces overall editorial quality.

And sometimes the laggards are the supervising editors. They forgo the time required to personally review all pages prior to publication. So goofs somehow get through, like the photo of five executives with a caption identifying four, or a paragraph that refers to 14 points, followed by list of 15. Some mishaps are laughable, like the reference to the United States that appeared as the "Untied States." These and other embarrassing typos are pointed out by top management or a gleeful salesperson, or even worse, by competitors who trumpet examples of your inept editing during a sales presentation.

Next let's consider the editor who says, "I have paid my dues." Any chief editor who believes this to be an earned status ends up being guilty of behavior that others will feel entitled to follow. "Sure, you come in at 8:30 AM, but get right to work," disgruntled junior editors used to tell me. "Our editor comes in at 8:30 too, but then spends the next hour conducting personal business with buddies." Or "Our editor always goes to lunch for three hours. What's going on?"

A related burnout signal is conveyed when the chief editor resists field trips. ("I'll only go to trade shows that I can't get out of attending. Otherwise, I'm going to delegate the trip to staff.") This is an attitude that will create resentment. Perhaps you are surprised to hear that travel assignments are not always a source of joy. In reality, staff members initially eager to travel learn that constant field trips are no picnic. (Of course, a different travel problem is when field trip budget is nonexistent. A staff that's chained to headquarter desks never fully grasps what the industry the publication serves really is all about.)

Finally, how about the mindset that rejects editorial coverage of advertisers? One known symptom of this pressure having reached a boiling point is when senior editors either bury advertiser complaints or rebuff salespeople's requests to make amends for alleged mishaps.

No matter what the circumstances, you need a policy for dealing with anything that could go wrong with respect to advertiser complaints. Typical questions your guidelines should cover include, "If the advertiser complained about lack of coverage during a sales call, how should the salesperson respond?" or, "How should the editor follow up?" The most important requirement for editors in this regard is to convey a positive attitude to advertisers seeking editorial support.

Helpful in this respect is preparing and circulating vendor guidelines for editorial coverage. At Gralla, we even offered a workshop for vendors focusing on coverage possibilities. Often held during a major convention, the session was always well-attended.

6

Fix Your Editorial Marketing Arsenal

W hen I complete competitive editorial analysis projects, I often find that the magazines or websites compared are almost evenly matched. Content delivery is consistently high-value, to the point where the project sponsor needs to revisit its editorial marketing strategy. Is every possible available tool in the editorial marketing arsenal used to enhance an image of clear superiority? If not, what additional promotion activity could be undertaken?

For example, during one recent matchup of B2B magazines, neither publication benefited from such assets as strong cover blurbs, timely analytical news reports, consistent statistical presentation, or a solid lineup of regular columnists covering a variety of management and marketing concerns.

The best way to introduce this discussion is by suggesting the use of my editorial marketing self-scoring profile. Editors and salespeople should tackle the exercise separately, then compare notes.

On the next page, you'll find a list of 10 possible marketing tools where the editor should be the key player in terms of creativity. Award a maximum score of 10 points for each tool if you always use it, five points if you sometimes use it, or zero points if you never use it. The top score is 100. You need 90 for a passing grade.

Editorial Marketing Factor	Score
Competitive analysis reports are done regularly.	
Weekly or monthly promotion newsletter combines "commercials" with hot, late-breaking exclusives.	
Slide shows give vendors and ad agencies a special advance look at key industry trends.	
Updated "editorial portfolio" confirms your publication's superiority.	
Editors play a major role during special calls on key accounts with or without the publisher or salespeople.	
Ideas for revenue-producing special projects such as advertorials, supplements, and webinars suggested.	
Convention issues are superior rather than run-of-the mill show previews and regular departments.	
Editors are reliable problem-solvers when fielding advertiser complaints.	
A standard feedback system keeps salespeople advised of editorial contact with key advertisers.	
Editors prepare and regularly update a "First-and-only" media kit insert.	
Total Score:	

My favorites among the items in the above list are the editorial portfolio, industry-trends slide show, and "first-and-only" insert. Let's take a closer look at each of these valuable tools for editorial marketing.

Showcase your editorial successes

The function of an editorial portfolio is to collect and showcase editorial achievement. When I describe this tool at sales meetings, the usual response is enthusiastic. But developing and updating the portfolio takes a lot of time. So it's not surprising that in 28 years of consulting, I have seen only two companies give this concept a shot.

There is a wide range of effective types of content that can be highlighted and excerpted in the portfolio:

- Editorial columns that drew a terrific response by hitting industry hot buttons.
- Reports on speeches given by editors at major industry events, or articles describing industry awards conferred on editors, or other evidence of industry involvement, such as sponsorship of new product development competitions.
- Excerpts from important exclusive research published in your magazine.
- Evidence of presence at industry events, such as coverage of conventions or key legislative hearings, especially when such events are widely scattered geographically.
- Evidence of articles demonstrating that your editors constantly make field trips. This is especially useful if your competitors' travel is limited.
- Proof of your close ties with industry movers and shakers, such as exclusive interviews with top executives of major corporations and associations.
- General indications of editorial leadership, such as overviews of how your publication or website deals with important industry issues such as research, or examples of columns or scoops where your editors addressed a critical development before any competitors.

Slide show demonstrates research excellence

Another very important component of an editorial marketing arsenal is the trends slide show. To bring this off, you need a vehicle—ideally statistically based—that ad agency and corporate types will regard as a must-see program. Included under this banner are talks an editor/publisher team could deliver at national sales meetings or closed-door sessions for select executive groups.

During my time at Gralla, the company bought a magazine that trailed competitors on all fronts. The acquired property had a promising vehicle—an annual study of industry expenditures—that had never been exploited properly. Over time, we created a yearly audiovisual presentation that landed dozens of speaking slots. How did we do it? We sent a special mailing to the entire promotion list alerting everyone about the program's availability. The show of interest—marked by dozens of invitations to present the slideshow—was immediate.

Although the presentation was intended to gain private audiences with customers and prospects, we had several requests to present a tailored version at important industry conventions. Our new, higher profile brought us into contact with customer top management. Gradually our publication became a formidable competitor for plum ad schedules.

'First' and 'only' are magic words

Consistently documenting that your editorial staff scoops the opposition translates into an excellent marketing edge. The vehicle for promoting this asset usually is a media kit insert listing several examples of your outstanding editorial enterprise. But if broadcasting a "first and only" message appeals to publishers, you must first determine what shape you are in to support that claim. During many training workshops, I issue an opening challenge to participants to devote five minutes to listing all recent examples of first and only accomplishments. More often than not, session attendees can conjure up only a meager response.

Finally, a less ambitious but still promising variation of an editorial portfolio is the creation of an annual "State of the

Industry" report that can be used as a handout during initial contacts with advertising prospects. The report also can be distributed to other folks researching your field and seeking input from an authoritative source.

7

How to Assess Editorial Superiority

Valid claims about editorial quantitative superiority should always be made during presentations to advertisers. Most publishers understand this, but perhaps don't go far enough in terms of mining their content for every possible edge. This is where editors can help.

Four key categories

Let's consider four data categories often overlooked when marketing teams are planning a competitive assault involving print or online media:

- The "Look Who's Talking" report
- Story-telling graphics
- The presence of zero-factor warning signs
- High-interest content in at-show issues

Let's review each of these categories and how they can be used to highlight your editorial chops—assuming you perform well in each.

Look who's talking. Every competitive analysis presentation should include what I call a "Look Who's Talking" report. The idea here is to show how your editors and reporters are reaching out to and quoting an impressive number and variety of targeted end-users. Some publications demonstrate impressive enterprise when it comes to gathering end-user comments. But far more do a so-so job at best.

Then you have an additional group of publications that pursue reader comment, but gather most of it from advertisers, associations, and other sources while virtually ignoring the end-user—the publication's key circulation category.

For many competitive analysis studies, I include a table in which people quoted in articles are listed by three types of reader: end-user (i.e., target readers), vendor (i.e., potential advertisers), and other (such as consultants, academic experts, and government officials).

Another competitive edge involving direct quotes may appear if you can determine that the opposition is not reaching out to the best sources. For example, a study I conducted for a regionally focused publication found that 65 percent of content was based on input from executives in the least important circulation categories. In another case, involving a publication focusing on marketing executives, the initial analysis confirmed that my client's editors managed to reach the best sources only 20 percent of the time. Instead, more than half the quotes they used were taken from PR announcements covering a range of unrelated topics.

Last but not least, competitive analysis often detects "source overkill." This phenomenon occurs when editors rely on quoting a limited number of "old friends." Knowing this about potential competitors is useful during the stage when you are planning a debut issue in a field where several opponents already exist. An alert editorial team can stand out from that competitor by establishing connections with a broader range of authoritative sources. This accomplishment can be translated into a useful strength worth exploiting immediately.

Based on several studies I've conducted, online news titles are particularly vulnerable to coming up short on end-user quotes. Out of 1114 quotes I found in two studies, only 392, or 35 percent, were from end-users. And of the 100 sites I examined, 22 carried no end-user quotes at all.

Story-telling graphics. When a typical magazine competitive analysis strategy is mapped out, the emphasis is usually on what the words say as opposed to how the information is illustrated. Thus editors may be asked to track the number of pages devoted to a specific important issue. Or attention might be paid to "first and only" achievements by competing publications.

Such approaches, of course, have merit. But adding graphics analysis to your package may suggest additional strengths worth exploiting or surprising weaknesses worth correcting. Let's look at five possible categories worth tracking for a test period of three to six months.

- *Overall illustrated percentage.* This category reflects the relationship between total pages per issue carrying editorial content and what percentage of those pages are illustrated with photos, line art, or tabular material.

- *Infographics percentage.* Instructive graphic elements should appear on at least 20 percent of pages carrying editorial content. Of the five factors addressed in this discussion, poor infographics execution is the most common shortcoming.

- *Graphics/page ratio.* This calculation requires dividing total number of pages carrying editorial into total number of illustrations. A sub-consideration of that relationship is there should be at least one graphic on every page carrying editorial content. The true standard of excellence would be a ratio of 2.0 or higher.

- *Number of active front-cover lines.* Cover lines using active verbs are stronger than verb-less label headlines. An attention-getting cover offers at least five active story lines covering a variety of topics. Some editors are able to include as many as eight active story lines.

- *Story-telling photos percentage.* While a magazine may be abundantly illustrated, many photos used lack news impact. For example, some publications are dominated by head shots and concept photos.

The latter are acceptable on occasion, but concepts too often involve overuse of stock art (like handshakes, dollar signs, over-sized question marks, and so forth). My photo analysis target therefore calls for faces or concepts to account for no more than 20 percent of illustrations in an issue. There are, of course, exceptions to this rule, such as an issue featuring a special industry personalities report.

Zero-factor warning signs. The competitive editorial strengths and weaknesses reports I produce for clients encompass 25 qualitative factors. Of these, there are 10 factors that should never earn less than a full score, whatever the rating system you use. I call these "zero factors" because anything less than a top score is equivalent to a zero. The presence of any of these zero factors should be regarded as critical warning signs for your editorial content:

1. *Editorial column impact.* Is the editor's column a product of original thinking or merely a recitation of the contents page? Does the column exude leadership or suggest that the author is unfamiliar with the industry and has no link to major players? A frequent flaw in these columns is the message—or lack thereof—the headline conveys. Message-less headlines typically result if the editor is chained to some restrictive design policy that dictates no headline run longer than two or three words.

2. *Chief editor visibility.* An important qualitative fault occurs when a publication's most knowledgeable editor rarely writes anything beyond a regular personal column. There is a perspective missing that may not readily be offset by contributions from subordinates, no matter what their expertise level. Equally damaging are those situations where the editor, in an effort to maintain visibility, bylines a humdrum article. A typical example of such subpar effort is an article consisting of a few opening paragraphs leading to a

series of rewritten product item descriptions based on press announcements.

3. *Frequency of news scoops.* How often does news coverage reflect investigative reporting or exclusives? Some publishers actually use "scoop analysis reports" comparing which editors first broke what hot story. This exercise is especially pertinent in the current online news environment that has rapidly progressed from weekly to daily frequency.

4. *Contents page boredom.* Do headings go beyond conventional labels such as "Features" and "Departments?" Are photos accompanied by newsy captions, not just the page number or even less than that? Do department listings include information about content in that issue, or are they made up of short, unchanging labels?

5. *Article reference value.* This is a two-part consideration based on presence of original research plus consistent use of infographic elements. The latter include charts, diagrams, and sidebars, with checklist or grid formats or step-by-step photo sequences. At least 20 percent of magazine pages carrying editorial content should use infographics.

6. *Coverage of movers and shakers.* To be successful, your editors must have excellent relationships with top executives at major corporations and associations. One sign of such relationships is a regular department using a question-and-answer format featuring industry players.

7. *Evidence of reader involvement.* If your content doesn't show signs of readers interacting with it, you've got a problem. Upgrading is possible by means of such editorial devices as problem-solving columns, IQ tests, e-mail and online-surveys, summaries of timely chat-room discussions, or other editorial content voluntarily contributed by readers.

8. *Geographic scope.* Is reader input drawn from

around the country or solely from a limited geographic area? For some projects a detailed direct-quote analysis based on at least six issues of your publication or website versus competitors provides useful data for a compelling promotion piece. This is a particularly potent weapon when directed at competitive staffs that spend most of their time interviewing suppliers and advertisers rather than core reader end-users.

9. *Variety of sources.* When analysis shows that editors quote the same sources in almost every issue, this factor earns zero points. A variation of this flaw is "source overkill." This happens when the same sources are quoted frequently in different articles within a single issue.

10. *Exciting last page.* How is the editorial page facing the back cover used? Creative editors make the most of this location by reserving it for an exciting department or column. Surprisingly, others still use it as a dumping ground for classified ads, the advertiser index, or a jump page for one or more articles.

Analyze show issues

If you do nothing else in the way of competitive analysis throughout the year, be sure to make comparison of your show issues with those of your competitors a regular event. (Just so it's clear, by *show issue*, I mean an issue of a magazine that is explicitly aimed at and distributed to the audience attending a trade show or conference.)

I learned the importance of comparing show issues during my first competitive analysis project. The vice president of sales asked me to evaluate one of our publications versus two tough competitors. My procedure was to read six issues—including two show issues—of each magazine.

The key finding for show issues was that we bulked them up largely with standard conference information, such as booth listings and an endless number of exhibit hall diagrams. By contrast, both of our competitors played down show information that was readily available in convention hall directories. As a result, they were able to devote much more space to interesting, high-value content for attendees to take away with them.

Clearly the focus on non-show content afforded a competitive edge to our opposition. So we resolved to change our approach. For future show issues, we greatly reduced the amount of what was once considered as "given" content. In its place, we offered an impressive number of articles with high take-away value. This was noticed and appreciated by many show attendees.

Our decision may sound like heresy to those publishers and editors who take the traditional approach to show issues. Over the years, I have maintained that there is no need to overload these key issues with standard convention details. Instead, use a pre-show issue for that purpose. Once you're at the show, the issue distributed there must emphasize your editorial strengths and resources.

8

Compete with Authority

As you put into practice the types of editorial competitive analysis described in the preceding chapter, you'll soon see the most important competitive advantage is genuine editorial authority. In this chapter, let's look at some effective ways to convey that authority and instill fear in your competitors.

Aim for insider status

Many editor-in-chief personal columns need to go the extra mile if the objective is to develop a loyal following. Where many editors fall short in this aim is that they produce editor's columns that show them to be *observers* rather than *insiders*. The best the observer can do is to describe a known industry problem, then leave readers to figure out best courses of action. The insider goes an important step further, by proposing solutions to the problem.

(Note that there is an all-too-common third status: "parroting." Typically the editor makes no attempt to introduce original thinking. Instead, the commentary pulls excerpts from articles appearing in the issue, becoming, in essence, a second contents page.)

Now consider this: for competitive analysis projects, I always start with the editorial column. You can punch some very big holes in the opposition's armor if columns do not exude the desirable insider aura. This is of special concern with debut issues. When you sponsor a launch, your goal is to demonstrate total editorial capability and deep information resources. You want to impress readers with authoritative content produced by an industry-savvy staff. Producing a debut issue like this will scare the dickens out of existing competitors that have been getting by with a minimum-value editorial package. By contrast, failing to show expertise in and understanding of the industry you're entering will allow your competitors to rip your effort to shreds. Alert competitors can detect when editors new to the industry are faking their savvy.

Dozens of factors come into play during the launch stage. First and foremost, the editorial column should reflect the editor-in-chief's knowledge of the industry. Using this column to make a humdrum announcement of the magazine's launch and inviting reader feedback is a waste of time.

A more dangerous practice in a first column, however, is to make unfulfilled promises about future editorial content. Smart competitors will save the debut issue's editorial column and, several issues down the pike, compare the promises made with the subsequent reality. If the publication has fallen short of its promises—as so many do—an itemized list of those shortfalls can do competitive damage.

So, assuming you really do have an insider's understanding of the industry you cover and lots of key connections, how do you show that in an editor's column? Here are a few effective approaches to take:

Use a distinctive name and logo. Columns that are identified only as "Editorial," "Editor's Page," or "From My Desk", and so forth, are a dime a dozen. Instead, select a name that somehow connects with the industry you cover and incorporate it into a distinctive logo.

Interpret current statistics. Rather stick to the opinion piece approach, some editors devote their regular columns to analyzing current data based on either original publication research or secondary source studies.

Stick out your neck. As each year concludes, offer half-a-dozen or so predictions of what lies ahead. In the same column, review how many predictions made during the previous year were on target.

Offer an IQ exam. This change-of-pace approach takes the form of a multiple-choice test assessing the reader's grasp of technical basics. Test-takers submit an answer sheet (you may want to offer an online option to make this easy). Congratulate the top 10 scorers in a subsequent column. The value of this approach is greatest, of course, in those cases where the majority of test-takers flunk the exam.

Avoid the "convention is coming' column. In this case, like clockwork, the editor's column in a show issue advises readers that —surprise!— the annual show is right around the corner. Readers are told to take advantage of networking opportunities, wear comfortable shoes, and follow other such sage advice. Blah! Instead, before writing a show preview column, network with a dozen solid contacts. Find out what's really on the industry's mind, and give your readers a welcome heads-up.

Of course, to convey an insider's authority effectively in an editorial, it helps to reflect expertise in the craft of writing as well. Here are a few suggestions that can help:

- The headline should immediately reflect the column's take-away value. Don't expect to do this with a format that requires headline lengths of just three or four words.

- If a deck is required by your format, it should expand upon rather than repeat the headline's message.
- The introductory paragraph should reach a key story point within the first 10 words. Obviously that's impossible if you are a fan of launching each column with a multi-paragraph anecdote lacking immediacy.
- Emphasize readability. The Fog Index reading level of the column should fall between grades 10 and 12. (If you aren't familiar with the Fog Index, read about it in the appendix to this book.) Big words and long sentences only obscure your authority. If you understand your topic well, make sure your reader will too.

A word about controversy

With authority comes a double-edged awareness of controversy. Addressing a controversy in an editorial column can demonstrate authority, but it is not without significant risks.

I recently learned of a fracas occurring when the editor of a consumer magazine took a stand contrary to widely held views of his audience. Readers were outraged and some corporate executives were incensed enough to cancel their advertising schedules. Ultimately, perhaps when backed into a corner, top management dismissed the editor.

The situation reminded me of my own brushes with controversial matters during my editorial career. To this day, I believe that every industry has important touchy issues that deserve attention. Some editors, supported by their publishers, have the courage to move ahead with commentary on these issues. But in too many cases, a publisher concerned that advertisers will be offended bludgeons his editor into silence. And there are other times when editorial staffs, buried in quantitative drudgery, have no time to pursue situations where important conflicting views exist.

As a result, in many of the editorial competitive analysis projects I've conducted, I have found multiple conflicts that are begging for coverage. That said, I have witnessed other moments when editors jumped the gun, basing an explosive personal column on unsubstantiated views from a lone individual with an obvious axe to grind.

Well-warranted controversy should have its day in every trade publication. If you agree, how do you decide which issues should be exposed? And if you disagree, you may not be delivering enough of the need-to-know information your audience has found it can obtain elsewhere.

Five editorial fear factors

"Preemptive discouragement of a direct competitor should be a key focus." This was the closing statement in an editorial planning report recently submitted by a top B2B editor to senior management. He added, "If I had to summarize our editorial focus, it is to raise the 'editorial bar' so high that it would be extremely difficult for a competitor to emerge."

Take it from me: this comment is on the money. The presence of strong editorial "fear factors" is always a focus when I evaluate existing publications serving a given market. My quest: find a situation where a start-up could vault my new magazine into a leadership position.

So how strong are your fear factors? Is your editorial leadership position sufficiently fortified to the point where potential competition trembles? Here are five practices that would shake my resolve if I were thinking about invading your field, especially if all of them are in play.

> **1. A high-profile editor-in-chief.** This individual always is sought out for speaking engagements at conventions sponsored by key industry groups. In every issue, he or she writes an important feature that reflects insider status. Editorial columns always address important issues as opposed to habitually parroting the contents page. In addition, several editorial staff members are active participants in association affairs, to

the point of being officers, directors, or committee heads.

2. A constant stream of original research. You can count on this publication to maintain a strong statistical presence throughout the year.

3. A generous travel budget. Editorial staffers seem to be everywhere. A new magazine with limited bucks to support field trips clearly wouldn't stand a chance. This fear factor alone would be sufficiently daunting for a potential competitor at a time when editorial budgets are so often severely constrained.

4. Dynamite show issues. Several blockbuster features are in the lineup. Event previews are enterprising, not just the typical combination of exhibitor lists, workshop blurbs, and expanded product item write-ups.

5. Authoritative columnists. Regular contributions from recognized industry experts reflect a solid knowledge of the field in question. These authors always provide charts or useful checklists. The value of these infographics is established when matched against typical "shotgun" columns that easily could appear in hundreds of other magazines.

One executive who reviewed my list commented in an e-mail on the value of making an investment in these fear factors:

"Before a publishing house gets too complacent, it has to acknowledge that a well-financed start-up organization can cause a lot of mischief by taking away share of market. A start-up can achieve four of the five factors right out of the blocks. If the potential start-up can woo a high-profile editor (unlikely?), then it achieves all five."

As I told my correspondent, it certainly is true that a well-financed new competitor could do immediate damage to an unwary, complacent organization. On the other hand, there are many new competitors who may be unwilling to go the extra mile, especially when it comes to editorial investment.

Meanwhile, some publishers already serving an existing market have yet to loosen up the financial belts they tightened several years ago. Those are the folks who could lose their race to a newcomer by default, even if the extra opposition isn't immediately four-star in the five editorial areas I've itemized. In fact, a three-star invader might easily prevail over incumbents whose editorial effort has drifted down to a two-star rating or less.

As an important aside, that vital high-profile editor-in-chief fear factor is starting to become elusive in some quarters. The B2B publishing industry needs to work harder at beefing up the leadership potential throughout the editorial line of succession.

9

Make the Most of Trade Shows

Industry conventions and trade shows provide an unmatched location for editors to gather information for both immediate publication and future story assignments. Moreover, with proper planning, an editorial staff can create a strong presence through such devices as conference presentations, show newspapers or "hotline" newsletters, and hospitality events coupled with an exclusive award presentation. And, of course, there are variations on all these themes.

Knowing this, one of my early clients, wise in many ways, asked me to prepare a document covering everything I could suggest that facilitated post-show reporting superior to that of most competitors. In those days, we didn't have video to rely on for immediate, high-impact reporting. Even so, this advice of yesterday clearly applies to today's efforts. So here are a few excerpts to get the ball rolling:

1. **Study how your opposition covers a convention.** Are articles based primarily on official remarks? Do editors conduct special interviews with key executives that are spin-offs of official proceedings? Are roundup interviews conducted on the exhibit floor with show attendees? Even though your competition may have more editors at a show, are some valuable seminars covered inadequately or totally ignored?

2. Related to the above point, check the degree to which competitive staffs hang out in the pressroom. At one point after applying this strategy to a show I had attended for two years, I found that my opposition actively conducted exhibit hall interviews but rarely covered some excellent management workshops. For the next few years, I had this coverage all to myself and my staff. We finally tipped our hand when our sales department ran a post-show promotion touting evidence of our exclusivity. The claim went undisputed, but the edge we enjoyed was wiped away.

3. Develop your own advance editorial plan for show coverage. Assuming that your study of the opposition shows many openings for exclusive coverage, you must decide on the vehicles that will give you the greatest advantage.

4. Create your own event. At least 90 days before the convention, select a hot topic along with a list of executives who might best address the issue. Your objective is to sponsor a luncheon or dinner panel discussion lasting approximately 90 minutes, including food service. Aim for no more than six panelists, so that show-goers can more easily keep track of the personalities being quoted when reading coverage of your event.

5. Take advantage of editorial advisory boards. If your board consists of 20 to 30 industry executives, and one of their acknowledged functions is a panel discussion scheduled during a major convention, panel organization should be easier. Of course, editorial boards serve many purposes, such as to review magazine direction and provide input on all surveys. If you don't have a board, consider organizing one when convention events are being planned. Hint: be sure your board member recruitment is as personalized as possible. An obviously mass-distributed e-mail blast should be avoided. (For more tips on using advisory boards, see "How to maximize editorial board feedback" in the appendix.)

Seven ways to maximize coverage

The reporting techniques you use at trade shows should be efficiency-oriented. Here are seven suggestions that may help improve coverage at your next event.

1. Always try to get your own angle on presentations. When a session that you're covering ends, catch the speaker for a few minutes of additional, exclusive comments. Lead off the story you write with the speaker's response to your queries, if it is interesting enough. Always come prepared with a few special questions that challenge the speaker's expertise.

2. Don't blindly recap the points of a speech in the order delivered. The most important part of the speech for your readers may not occur until the middle or end of the talk. If so, lead with the important material; plan to exclude stuff you may have covered before.

3. Don't use a tape recorder unless you really need it for backup. Transcribing a tape can be extremely time-consuming. You'll finish your article much faster, especially if a 30-45-minute talk is involved, if you work from detailed notes. The best way to approach note taking is as if you are taking dictation. Get everything down word-for-word; since it's probably not all gospel, you'll have breathing space to keep up. Write as small as possible; it will be easier to take down the salient comments in full.

4. The question-and-answer period can often make up the bulk of your coverage. Some writers assigned to an event stick around for the official speech, then tune out during the Q&A. Also, always be aware of outspoken audience members. These folks may be your best source of an exclusive.

5. Be a visible photographer. Always sit in the front row of the hall so you can snap your shots without disturbing too many people in the audience. When photographing several speakers at a single session, shoot each person from different angles. This gives you more leeway for a subsequent graphic presentation. Arrive early and try to photograph speakers before the program starts. If possible, pose the panelists and ask them to gesture for your shots. They will usually cooperate.

6. When covering a distant event, try to add-on a visit to an industry leader's facility. You may be able to arrive a day earlier or stay a day later for this purpose.

7. Write your articles as soon as possible after the event. If the event requires air travel, and you have time to kill at the airport or on the plane, attempt some first drafts. Obviously, the sooner you finish your articles, the less you will need to rely on fading recall later on.

Speaking? Prepare well

There's nothing worse than landing a conference speaking slot you've always wanted, then blowing it because you weren't prepared or sound as if you're reading every word.

Here are eight suggestions on how to hurdle the speaking barrier:

1. Time your presentation. Learn how to estimate whether or not your prepared remarks will get the job done. If you work from a script that is single-spaced, for example, it could be that each page equals five minutes of time at your formal speaking pace.

2. Be prepared to talk without reading directly from a text. This doesn't mean that you have to memorize your remarks. What it does mean is that if you are working with slides, you should create a storyboard that allows the slides to function as your script.

3. Prepare a handout to accompany your presentation. No matter how small your audience, a leave-behind is worth the effort.

4. Don't be trite at the outset of your talk. "It's nice to be here" ranks with "May I help you" or "Have a nice day" as a stimulating warm-up. Instead, be startling. Tell a joke, make fun of yourself, or put some imagination into your first few audiovisuals.

5. Make your availability known. Even though you may be invited to speak without prompting on your part, it always pays to let the industry you cover know that you are available and can do a terrific job.

6. Find the right presentation format. Don't assume there's only one way to speak at an event. Consider all the possibilities. One effective setup for a convention presentation is to have the publisher or editor serve as the panel moderator and round up panelists. Alternatively, the publisher or editor may make a solo speech to unveil findings of important publication research. There are endless variations you can explore.

7. Combine hospitality with editorial publicity. If your magazine runs a hospitality party during a major show, consider how you can convert it into an editorial event. One approach is for your publication to announce some form of editorial awards competition before the show. The winners can be recognized during your event at the upcoming convention.

8. Put on a tournament. Another possibility is to sponsor a recreation event, such as an after-hours tennis tournament, with winners announced in your post-convention issue. The success of such an undertaking will vary by industry. And, of course, it helps if your staff includes some competent tennis players, so they can be more directly involved in the competition.

Test your trade show savvy

Now that we've discussed some of the ways you can get more out of the trade shows you cover, it's time to assess your own event savvy with the following self-scoring profile. Don't worry if your score is lower than you'd like—in the process, you will identify areas to work on to improve your trade show success.

Before you put the self-scoring profile to use, you must decide which coverage factors require the most improvement in the publication in question. They will be worth either 15 or 10 points. Practically speaking, you probably can have just one 15-point factor and three 10-point factors if you wish to stay within a grand total of 100 points. Of course, you also can change the emphasis by raising the maximum score.

Required action	Score
Plan ahead to decide who covers which event and how many articles each editor writes.	
Always seek exclusivity. Base some assignments on action occurring beyond the formal program.	
Video cameras are required. Editors are highly visible and active photographers.	
Create your own event. Panel discussions, full-blown side shows, award presentations or booth surveys are among the options.	
Provide ample space in the next available issue or e-mail newsletter to demonstrate strong staff presence at the event.	
Offer a series of mini-stories rather than one long wrap-up article.	
Chronological reporting of a speech occurs only if the speaker conveys key points at the outset.	
If a speech is general or old hat, buttonhole the speaker later for more significant input.	
For some preview reports, gather advance comment from several key speakers.	
Show preview headlines reflect an editor's ability to go beyond the obvious.	
Write as much wrap-up copy as possible during the show, while the best angles are fresh in mind.	
Include articles requiring exhibitor feedback.	
Send timely follow-up thanks to helpful sources.	
Conduct interviews for articles that run at a later date.	
Include "picture pages" in post-show layout.	
Total Score:	

10

Go All Out for Debut Issues

Not every debut issue is destined to succeed. Why? Publishers and editors underestimate the dedication required to stand out in a crowd of existing competitors. When I discuss debut issue strategy with clients, my initial focus is on 20 editorial factors. The first 10 are given particularly high priority.

1. Editorial page count. Paramount among the high-priority group of factors is having at least 50 editorial pages. Every so often, I am asked to comment on a client's effort that includes a much lower page count. Big mistake, I stress, especially if existing competitors have made a substantial editorial investment. A recent study conducted of 10 debut issues found only three in the ballpark in terms of preferred page count. Another three ran fewer than 40 pages.

2. Number of end-user direct quotes. The scoring system I apply to debut issue performance includes a special consideration for the use of authoritative direct quotes. Historically, an ongoing B2B weakness in print and online has been an inability to reach out to end-user sources. The presence of 15 or more end-user quotes (as opposed to a mix of quotes from vendors, associations, and other sources) earns a top score in my analyses. In most of the issues I studied, editors settled for interviewing other types of sources who were more easily reached than end-users.

3. Original research capability. Six debuts lacked any original research. A debut issue should include an article containing original statistics. If your company already publishes a magazine serving the field in question, pull your sample from the existing circulation list. The study you create can be a single page. Be sure to refer to the resulting article in an attention-getting cover blurb.

4. Editor-in-chief's column. The editorial column should reflect the author's industry knowledge. A conventional announcement focusing on the magazine's launch is unacceptable.

5. Outstanding cover story. Create a feature article written by the editor-in-chief that addresses a timely trend. The article should be solutions oriented, and based on input from a dozen or more recognized industry leaders. It should include several sidebars plus appropriate infographics such as charts or checklists.

6. Recognized authoritative sources. Authoritative sources are association executives, prominent vendors, and the acknowledged industry movers and shakers among end-users. There should be clear evidence that editors are in touch with leading lights through interviews or recruitment as contributing editors.

7. Infographics. At least 25 percent of the editorial pages in a debut issue should include them (for regular issues, 20 percent is okay). Only one issue I studied reached the target; five used few or no infographics.

8. Involvement devices. These editorial elements invite readers to contribute content by responding to e-mail polls, problem-solving columns, quizzes, contributing education opportunities, or contests. Of the 10 issues I studied, seven offered no involvement devices.

9. Feature written by top editor. Five of the debut issues I reviewed lacked an important feature by the editor-in-chief. A common policy oversight—especially where debut issues are concerned—finds the only contribution from the top editor to be a standard one-page column. Instead, plan a lead article that reflects the editor's insider status by connecting with leading industry sources. Devote at least six full pages to the editor's contribution.

10. Editorial advisory board in place. Eight of the reviewed issues had not yet organized an editorial board. Establishing a board may be difficult to achieve immediately unless your potential pool of members is familiar with other magazines you publish. But if your preliminary research includes a careful editorial review of at least a dozen issues of each existing competitor, you can draw up a target list of potential board members. It's also possible to have your debut issue include an insert inviting high-profile readers to become valued board members.

Editorial basics should be well-executed

Now let's turn to the remaining 10 debut issue factors and best practices for executing them. In fact, there are simple ways—sometimes overlooked by competitors—to make these elements stand out.

11. Front page cover lines. Include four or more active headlines on the cover reflecting debut issue scoops.

12. Informative contents page. Avoid standard subject labels such as News, Features, and Departments. Instead, create headings that reflect the top concerns of readers.

13. Format variety. There are at least 30 possibilities to choose from.

14. Timely news section. Stop running rewrites of items that already appeared on your website. Try for a more analytical flavor.

15. Exciting last editorial page. Don't use this page as a repository for an ad index plus a few classified ads. Instead, reserve it for a high-interest, trends column.

16. Extensive four-color graphics. Blow away the competition with the use of color. The ideal would be a fully illustrated issue with four-color graphics on every page. But that's rare; 80 to 90 percent is more likely.

17. Authoritative columnists. Provide how-to content that is clearly unavailable elsewhere.

18. Editing skill (especially headline writing). In particular, you should always use active headlines; when possible, include attention-getting numbers.

19. Sidebar quality. Sidebars should include a graphic whenever possible. In addition, your format policy should stress the need for one or more sidebars per feature article.

20. Organized content flow. Create a content sequence that drives readers from an exciting up-front news section through high-interest features and then onward to a high-value products review section. Decide whether the editor-in-chief's personal column is better placed up front or on the last editorial page.

Start early; plan advance field trips

In the pre-online world, planning and executing a debut publication was an excitement-packed experience. I joined a B2B publisher to help launch a fifth magazine—in tabloid format—after which I participated in five more tabloid debuts within a short time period. The pace of launches in the B2B arena has slowed somewhat since those days. However, the editorial principles of yore still apply when it comes to assessing possible weaknesses among existing competitors. To that end, here are five factors your debut agenda should take into account:

1. Start working early on a preview issue. The new editor-in-chief should be in place at least five to six months before the preview is published. That issue should reflect a broad scope of coverage that highlights editorial strengths that may be executed poorly by existing opposition.

2. Make frequent field trips to meet recognized industry authorities. If you have not budgeted for this important editorial investment, you risk publishing content that exudes guessing-game flavor.

3. Obtain and read a year's worth of competitors' back issues. Among other benefits, this thorough review helps you identify the industry's news cycle. You need to be aware of all national and regional events that merit coverage and determine how you could do it better.

4. Identify competitors' editorial limitations. For example, is geographic coverage truly national or restricted to sources closer to home? Is there evidence of source overkill, where editors repeatedly interview the same small group of contacts?

5. Your preview issue chief editor's column must reflect a grasp of industry concerns. Do not make the mistake I've seen often in debuts where the editor does no more than state, in effect, "we are here to serve you."

11

Frequent Research Must Be a Priority

Without regularly published research, any claim to editorial superiority lacks merit. Of course it helps if you have an in-house research department to help further your cause. But even without this edge, you still can publish a stream of high-value statistical content. Any B2B publication seeking to build a reputation as an authoritative source invests heavily in its own capabilities as well as in partnerships with major market research companies. The benefit for readers is up to hundreds of thousands of dollars of free statistical material.

The following 14 questions may prove helpful to ask yourself if you are developing or revising your editorial research program.

1. What original research could you run in every issue?

2. How about secondary research? What regular sources exist?

3. If you use original or secondary data, can it take the form of a "last editorial page" column?

4. How will you extract the most data from each completed study?

5. What pros and cons apply when publishing brand-preference data? Can you offer tailored presentations during executive sessions conducted for current advertisers or prospects?

6. How can you increase infographics use? You should aim for having infographics on at least 20 percent of your total pages per issue carrying editorial content.

7. Will you always publicize survey results through an aggressive e-mail PR program?

8. How long will it take to create at least one dynamite original study that becomes a highly respected annual event?

9. How often do you run mini-polls on your website?

10. Can you conduct a survey from your booth at a major convention?

11. Are there industry associations that would partner with you on a joint study?

12. Can you make deals with respected research organizations, exchanging data for PR exposure?

13. Do you regularly gather reader preference data via A-B-C studies? (A = high interest; B = modest interest; C = no interest.)

14. What opportunities do you have to present survey results at an important national or regional convention?

Now here are 13 practices to keep in mind pertaining to creating and promoting original research:

1. Use editorial board members to help you create surveys.

2. Copy accompanying a survey summary should interpret data—not just recite it.

3. When presenting salary data, use medians rather than means. Always include regional analysis in the article.

4. Build cross-reference potential into your survey questions.

5. Leave questionnaire space for open-ended comments.

6. Promise anonymity unless respondents waive that right.

7. Consider including a tailored cover letter and personal note to key people you wish to respond.

8. Include attention-getting numbers in the headline and deck of the article summarizing survey results.

9. For most charts, be sure to include headings or captions that explain data significance.

10. Ask historical questions that yield data reflecting significant upturns or declines.

11. Test the clarity of table headings: see if other staff members understand what the charts and graphs actually show.

12. Don't assume that the secondary data used to develop a trends article is correct. Recalculate all figures.

13. Always confirm that the colors selected for tables will be distinguishable when the article prints or goes online.

Editors must be data-savvy

At Gralla Publications, we published more than 100 studies per year. These ranged from highly comprehensive consumer expenditure reports to analyses of reader business practices.

In the interests of data excellence, the company ran periodic "Math Facts for Editors" workshops led by our research director. The session included a challenging quiz covering salary study flaws, percentage increases versus percentage point increases, means versus medians, small-cell pitfalls, and plenty of other elusive stuff.

Here are a few excerpts from an "Editorial Research Whiz Special IQ Test" we developed:

- In 1991, there were 11.6% more hospital physical therapy (PT) units than in 1990. In 1992, there were 14.7% more hospital PT units than in 1991. Based on this data, is it true or false that the increase reported from 1991 to 1992 was 3.1% higher than the increase reported from 1990 to 1991?

- The following facts were reported in a survey of lawn care firms:
  o Of 1,000 firms surveyed, 18% responded
  o Of those responding, 48% also provide pest control services
  o Of those offering pest control services, 27% consider the business unsuccessful
  o The lack of success was attributed to high cost of service by 8% of respondents, to dissatisfied customers by 4%, and to a diminishing customer base by 4%.

  What common statistical problem is reflected by the use of these figures?

- In a recent survey conducted by a distributor magazine, readers were asked to rank several aspects of manufacturer service. Some of the resulting averages appear below (the lower the score, the more important the factor).
  o Accuracy of order fulfillment: 4.85
  o Delivery time: 5.26

     o   Responsiveness to inquiries: 5.85
     o   Spare parts availability: 6.94
     o   Turn-around time on repairs: 8.38
     o   Training: 9.10
     o   Contract maintenance: 12.03

Comments?

(And those were the easy questions. How did you make out?)

12

Overcoming Sponsored Content Hurdles

Today's publishing business clearly requires a constant flow of commercially exploitable editorial projects. Many firms have made special projects into a thriving concern. But such activities easily fizzle if creative ideas are not forthcoming. This reality has become considerably stronger thanks to the rising popularity of sponsored content as an advertising vehicle.

Publishers are relying more heavily on editorial input as a source of creative ideas for sponsored content. Editors who don't rise to the occasion may believe they are preserving some prerogative. But in reality, they are dampening their own future.

Being able to offer solid sponsored content recommendations is more likely if you have a grasp of some basics. Among other matters, your knowledge should cover possible formats, promotion strategy, and contractual requirements.

Six formats to consider

In practice, I've found the following six formats to be effective vehicles for sponsored content. Note that for any of these formats, senior editors should not write any ad copy. But it's good business to have an authoritative editorial manager participate in the initial pitch for sponsored content projects. For smaller firms, the editor-in-chief may be required to supervise a qualified writer. Former editorial staff members of the publication involved are the best choice.

1. Multiple sponsorship of an editorial supplement where no overt editorial exposure is offered.
2. Multiple sponsorship of an editorial supplement where advertisers are guaranteed direct exposure by being quoted or cited in some other way.
3. Show-in-print multiple sponsorship where there is an outright swap of editorial for advertising. In other words, advertisers receive a full-page editorial in exchange for buying a full-page ad. Smaller ads net more modest editorial space. At the outset, advertisers are offered the option of creating their own copy or having a publisher-provided freelance writer develop the content. (In my experience, the most surprising aspect of this format was the number of advertisers who, given the opportunity for editorial exposure, could not come up with anything when interviewed by my writers. In those cases, a consultation was required to pump the contact for possible editorial direction.)
4. Single sponsorship of an advertorial of any length. Advertisers should be reminded that to the degree possible, the content should be commercial-free.
5. Single sponsorship of an editorial project such as a survey or conference report.
6. Single sponsorship of a series of newsletters with a how-to theme. Of all the formats in the supplement or special-issue category, newsletters offer the most potential. In many cases, advertisers write their own copy. Undoubtedly there are many other firms that don't have those creative resources, but could be sold on the newsletter format as an advertising vehicle.

Launching a promotional campaign

Here is a four-step approach for launching a campaign designed to attract sponsored-content projects. Editors as well as salespeople should be involved in planning the action.

1. Create a prospect list of two dozen companies that have the budget for a bigger project and that have special knowledge or are engaged in marketing activity that has clear editorial merit. It is possible to cover several themes in a single section, depending upon available page count.
2. Create a comprehensive promotion piece to support your sponsored content effort. This piece must provide space to describe the editorial thought invested in the project. For example, a creative team meets with the client to brainstorm projects. The client is advised that several opportunities to review content will be scheduled. Also noted: Although staff senior editors are not involved in content creation, they supervise the project closely.
3. Come up with a "live" dummy of four to eight pages to demonstrate the dynamic flow of editorial material and various opportunities for ad placement.
4. Offer a merchandising package, such as a special advance mailing to key customers alerting them to the pending section, a reprint package, or maybe even a free ad in a prior issue announcing that this exciting supplement is coming soon.

When planning your campaign, it's important to be familiar with existing publishing industry guidelines. For instance, most stress that the sponsored content must not use the same graphic format as regular editorial content. Further, all advertising content must be clearly labeled as such on every page.

(The rise in recent years of "native advertising," which closely simulates regular editorial content, set off regulatory fireworks that eventually subsided. Consumer media seemed less concerned about graphic overlap with editorial than B2B media. The American Society of Business Publication Editors ethics committee, for instance, has taken a very strong stand against such overlap.)

Performance contract required

Bringing a sponsored content project to fruition can be hazardous. When I oversaw a special issues operation, clients backed out at the last minute on several occasions. As a result, we introduced a contract, realizing that it might not be honored. But at least we had a chance to review guidelines during a presentation. Our contract covered five areas:

1. What expense will and will not be incurred by the publisher. For instance, the publisher agrees to provide standard editorial photography. But if the client requires more elaborate art (such as still life, four-color shots of two dozen new products), the client will provide such photography.

2. Where case histories are called for, the client is responsible for all arrangements involving testimonials. That is, the client makes the deal with the customers to be quoted and handles all editorial clearances. This means that the client provides the publisher with written sign-offs on all editorial testimonial material to be used in the sponsored content.

3. One client contact is designated to be the liaison for the project. If multiple client clearances are involved, it is the contact's role to facilitate this process.

4. The approval process is outlined in detail. The client is advised that approval is based on a multi-stage schedule; the client's okay of each stage is final. For example, once the client has approved copy and is reviewing layouts, he or she cannot decide then to make wholesale copy changes.

5. Cancellation privileges and penalties are spelled out. This is a most troublesome area. Some publishers will allow an advertiser to terminate the project without cause. This translates into a forfeit of several thousand dollars of investment. Are you willing to do likewise? If not, where do you draw the line?

13

Five Challenges to Stellar Online News

A ny evaluation of online news capability must be considered in terms of competitive achievement. Columnists claiming expertise in online news matters emphasize the urgency of delivering high-value information unavailable elsewhere. Clearly this is a tall order. Let's take a look at some of the ways you can improve your online news delivery.

Five keys to better online news

Exclusivity is one of five key factors that are frequently found wanting in competitive comparison. The other four factors often fumbled are evidence of enterprise reporting, end-user input, embedded links, and skillful execution of editing basics.

Aim for exclusivity. Instead of exclusive news, competitive sites often post coverage of the same events, with embarrassing duplication in terms of angles chosen and sources quoted. Industries with constant breaking news have a better shot of providing an impressive flow of exclusive reporting. Other sites are not as fortunate. They don't have staff support required to dig behind the scenes for articles based on investigation rather than rewrites of low-interest PR announcements.

Imagine the frustration heaped upon a staff struggling to produce a weekly e-newsletter where industry news flow is anemic. Suddenly, the same staff is summoned to fulfill content demands for a second weekly or even a daily. Exclusivity here is almost out of the question. Instead the pipeline will be filled with old news where initial posts occurred on other sites weeks or months ago.

Convention coverage poses the true test whereby competitors should be able to document exclusivity. Who did the best job of interviewing program speakers as opposed to writing a story based on a PR handout? Who sponsored a newsworthy, well-attended event? How many end-users attending the show were polled for several roundup articles?

Publishers cannot support exclusivity claims by relying on curated material, no matter how timely. Making a favorable impression also is unlikely if most of a site's posts are unedited PR announcements. The best way to assess your competitive status in the race for exclusivity bragging rights is to compare how you and your competitors covered the same stories over the past three to six months. In many cases you may find your staff being outgunned by a competitor's more resourceful crew.

Show evidence of enterprise. A news story reflects enterprise if there is evidence that the author gathered exclusive information beyond what was provided in a press release. Examples of such evidence include statements that information was gathered from a source either during a telephone interview or an e-mail exchange.

Such declarations are missing from online news stories more often than not. So even if enterprise was involved when acquiring direct quotes, an observer could just as well assume that the comment was extracted from a PR announcement.

When you have used enterprise to gather exclusive quotes, make it clear in the story. A good model of how to confirm enterprise can be found in wording offered by the latest BuzzFeed editorial guidelines:

> "All quotes are to be attributed. Quotes that have been given directly to a BuzzFeed News staffer

should be noted as such by using the words 'told BuzzFeed News' at least once in the story."

In five studies of B2B online news delivery that I've conducted, a common thread was a lack of enterprise in 65 percent of the articles reviewed. A sixth study I completed in 2016 revisited 47 sites that earned at least 60 points during a previous study. Data covering B2B online news delivery by 43 sites showed 38 percent of articles provided no evidence of enterprise. Another 47 percent earned a low score, usually reflecting single-source input. Another way to consider this group's performance is that only 15 percent of articles involved better-than-average investigative effort.

Increase end-user quotes. Editorial staff success in gathering end-user quotes becomes a potent weapon during competitive analysis presentations. Even the best of the best are vulnerable, to judge from my studies. In the sixth study, the total number of direct quotes gathered was 536, of which 210, or 37 percent, were obtained from end-users.

To assess whether this ratio was acceptable, I applied a new end-user visibility (EUV) formula. The methodology involved called for scoring 10 articles per site on the designated review date. It seemed reasonable to assume that those 10 articles could collectively include 10 end-user quotes. This allows for the reality that not every article might be end-user sourced. So, a 10-article review that reached the target could post a 1.0 average. However, of the 43 responding sites, only four managed EUV of 1.0 or higher. Twenty-one sites recorded an EUV of less than 0.5.

Obviously some end-user basics are worth reviewing. Many publications demonstrate impressive enterprise when it comes to gathering comments from end-users. Just as many obviously do a so-so job. Another group pursues reader comment but gathers most of it from advertisers and other vendors. The end-user group—the publication's dominant circulation category—is virtually ignored.

A competitive edge may exist in the use of direct quotes if you find that the opposition doesn't interview the best sources. Before assessing what the opposition does or does not do, you must first assess how well you are performing in gathering quotes from the most authoritative contacts.

Improve embedded link quality. When I launched my B2B online news delivery study series in 2011, the number of embedded links was surprisingly low. Of 50 sites I reviewed annually between 2011 and 2015, nine out of 10 among the lowest-scoring news packages used no links. Another finding was that consumer media did a superior job in terms of offering high-quality links.

Seeking a more accurate B2B assessment, I introduced a link-usage visibility (LUV) calculation. The methodology premise is similar to the end-user visibility calculation described previously. In a nutshell, the minimum target for 10 articles scored per site should be at least one link per article, or an LUV of 1.0.

For 2015, the top 10 sites in this category averaged an LUV of 5.7. But that accomplishment was somewhat misleading. Of the collective 57 links used by the top ten, 34 came from just three sites, for a 3.4 LUV. This left the remaining seven sites with a lower 2.1 LUV. Meanwhile, the 10 lowest-scoring sites collectively posted a grand total of only one link, for a 0.1 LUV.

Shifting to 2016 results for 43 sites scoring 60.0 or higher in previous studies, the top 10 showed an average LUV of 22.7. The bottom 10 earned a 14.2 LUV; 13 sites among the 43 failed to attain the 1.0 minimum LUV. So it appears that B2B sites are not completely on board yet with acceptable embedded linking practices.

Note that in addition to the quantitative targets, there are qualitative considerations for links. For example, many high-scoring sites post links of several words summarizing link significance. Others settle for a single word. And there are cases where links send readers to information unrelated to the main article.

Focus on three editorial basics. When I score online news sites during consulting assignments, I might make allowances for heavy workloads due to daily frequency or lack of adequate staff support. But when it comes to newswriting basics, there are no excuses for foggy writing, lack of depth, or slow-developing introductory paragraphs. Nevertheless, many sites miss the boat in this regard, leaving themselves much more vulnerable to their competition. Here is a quick refresher covering three basic practices you probably could improve immediately.

Foggy writing. The Fog Index is a well-established readability measure I rely on when making judgments about editorial pace. Briefly, here's how Fog Index grade level calculations work (for more detail, see the appendix). First, you determine the average sentence length (ASL) of a passage of text. Next you find the percentage of "hard" words (HWP—generally three syllables or longer). Add the ASL and HWP, then multiply by 0.4 to find the grade level. The desired grade level is between 10 and 12. For B2B projects, it's okay to stretch the grade level to 12.5. In my analyses, articles within that range earn a full score of 10 points. Articles fogging out at 16 or higher earn zero points.

Evidence of depth. If article delivery draws primarily on 200- to 400-word rewrites of PR announcements, you'll rarely be able to offer insights afforded by, say, 1200 words. Some staffed-up sites develop several long-form articles daily. But if that's beyond you, at least the opening article should clearly reflect in-depth enterprise reporting as well as exclusivity. When

I apply my eight-factor scoring system during annual studies, in-depth coverage usually stands out in a crowd of lesser efforts.

Fast-paced lede. Introductory paragraph efficiency reflects the number of words used before reaching the "take-away" value of reader benefit. The fewer the words used, the better. An article reaching the key point within 10 words earns a full ten-point score. The key pitfall that often produces a zero score is the "source first, news second" format. This format is often used in PR announcements. Many editors allow this sequence because time doesn't allow "news first, source later" reconstruction.

What TV can teach us about online news

Occasionally TV show programming offers take-away value for B2B publishers. One of my favorite programs offering instructive value, *House of Cards*, always includes asides spoken by lead actor Kevin Spacey as he looks at the camera. Through these asides to the audience, he gives us input about his thoughts and where the current episode is heading.

Spacey portrays an astute politician scheming his way to become president of the United States. In the midst of his latest plot, he interrupts program flow for a quick chat with the audience about his intentions. There may be other shows that use this technique, but *House of Cards* was the first time I saw the approach in action during a TV drama. It works for me! And for some reason, it reminded me of a rarely seen online news technique I usually mention during my online news workshops.

The example that I use involves a B2B online news site relying on aggregated news. But instead of the traditional summary linking to each article, the editor takes an original approach. In the midst of the standard blurb, he expresses his view on the development in paragraphs set in red type.

Similarly, a few years ago, a brand-new site serving a high-tech audience posted an editorial side comment in almost every article. It used the format of a "WHAT TO DO" call-out advising readers about why and how they should respond to the development being covered. (Though it may not be common, this approach is not new. When I was an editor at a leading book publisher's news service division, the company used a call-out box in every article to liven things up.)

One more thing about the WHAT TO DO approach: it works better if, like Spacey's character, you've achieved industry insider status. That way, the reader is more likely to value your added insights.

Another instructive TV personality is Bill Maher, who once skewered news networks for the lack of take-away value offered in the lead story. "Every night it's the same thing," he growled, "a couple of minutes at the top on the big story of the day." After that, he said, all the networks waste their remaining time on innocuous coverage.

What should B2B news managers learn from Maher's criticism? Many B2B sites present online news in the same way as those networks. Yes, we have some winners who go all out to provide in-depth coverage of important developments. But in more cases, we rarely present that "big story of the day" in adequate depth. Instead, we have wall-to-wall, low-grade PR announcement rewrites.

So there is an obvious incentive for many B2B publishers to rise above the opposition by upgrading the true impact of news articles they deliver. Those who don't may end up being skewered—not so much by Bill Maher as by alert competitors.

10 interview pitfalls to avoid

My ongoing online news studies consistently observe a shortage of direct quotes in articles. Those quotes that do appear are not based on personal contact between editor and source. Instead, the information is close to a word-for-word rewrite of press announcements. As a result, the story often is hard to read, with lots of long sentences and low-value puffery. In the interests of upgrading direct-quote delivery, here are reminders of 10 pitfalls to avoid when conducting interviews for on-line and print articles:

1. Numberless pitfall. The interviewer settles for adjectives from his source ("big," "substantial," "modest") as opposed to hard numbers. Sometimes this occurs because the writer doesn't know the right questions to ask. At Gralla, we defeated this problem by requiring all editorial managers to provide staff with an interviewing checklist of questions requiring quantitative answers.

2. Transitional pitfall. After responding to the specific question posed by the interviewer, the source tacks on a totally unrelated observation that somehow gets posted.

3. Jargon pitfall. The source answers questions in popular terms (such as a fashion retailer talking about "functional" garments) but offers no specific examples.

4. Redundant pitfall. In the published article, a paraphrased point is followed by a quote that merely echoes, rather than expands upon, the initial comment.

5. Unclear pitfall. The writer does not understand what the source is saying but includes the direct quote anyway, assuming the editor or managing editor will catch mistakes.

6. Windbag pitfall. The source offers long-winded but low-value responses to most questions. The intimidated interviewer makes no attempt to channel the responses along more useful lines.

7. "For example" pitfall. The source generalizes about specific trends or techniques. The writer does not ask more "for example" or "what's new" questions in pursuit of better information.

8. Hype pitfall. This usually occurs during interviews with advertisers trying to insert as many self-serving statements as possible into the article.

9. Platitude pitfall. Typical-response quotes are used all too often in the story (like "people are our most important asset" or "quality products and services are emphasized at all times").

10. Wrong source pitfall. This usually shows up in articles based on end-user input. Because of difficulty in reaching the best source, writers settle for a convenient quote provided by a company PR source not necessarily in the loop. This habit needs breaking. Among other reasons, your opposition can use it against you in a competitive analysis report.

14

Twelve Ethical Issues You Must Address

What's your most pressing editorial ethics issue today? Due to the spate of election media hijinks in 2016, "fake news" might be your immediate response. At the same time, perhaps your current fact-checking policy is not the best. Of course, you could be correct on both accounts. But plenty of other ethics bumps on the editorial road are not easily smoothed over. Based on my time as ethics committee chairman of the American Society of Business Publication Editors, here are six ethical issues that may be looming somewhere in your future:

1. Trade show sponsor monkey business. Some show management groups continue to conjure up ways to squeeze B2B publishers for favorable editorial coverage. In one case, magazines were told they would be barred from attending a major industry event unless they provided an ample amount of favorable show coverage. But not all shows are winners; don't you owe it to your readers to report the debacles when they occur?

2. Exaggerated claims of inaccuracy. This is sort of an old story; it just hasn't received very much coverage. The typical scenario finds a recently interviewed source who is allowed to preview an article and then insists that it is totally inaccurate. The story must be pulled . . . or else! Many times such claims are a smoke screen. The true reason for the complaint may border on the bizarre. How will you handle this predicament?

3. Sponsored content integrity stretched to the limit. Many publishers have organized separate departments to create paid advertising content in an editorial format. Others are not so fortunate. Instead, full-time editors have to cope with extra responsibility of creating sponsored articles. And it's not surprising to find salespeople pressuring editors to bend integrity rules. How will you deal with that?

4. Fragile editorial quality. It seems like yesterday that the chairman of a prominent B2B publisher uttered his "we have become less good" admission during a packed workshop. That concern has been echoed many times over by respondents to some of my past polls. Accepting this decline in editorial quality flies in the face of ethics policy mandates—often located front and center in existing ethics codes. True, there are many explanations for disappointing quality, but much of it ultimately results from an absence of adequate top management support. Results of my own B2B online news performance studies consistently find that about two-thirds of articles posted reflect no evidence of enterprise.

5. Request to "unpublish." ASBPE called this matter to everyone's attention via an alert in our Ethics News Updates newsletter. If you've not yet established a policy for dealing with this issue, don't wait too much longer. Generally speaking, requests to "take down" an item should be denied, but there are exceptions.

6. Do-no-harm decisions. Speeches delivered at major events clearly are on the record. But sometimes an executive seeking to be a straight shooter on a touchy topic goes too far in telling the truth. If published, the information could severely damage the individual's career. Should you follow a path of "the truth must be told no matter what"—or give the messenger a pass in terms of publicizing some ultra-critical comments? On various occasions, I have asked speakers or people I am interviewing whether they wish to be on the record with what really amounts to newsworthy comments. What would you do in a similar situation?

The nagging nature of the six ethical issues described above is clearly confirmed in the introductory paragraph of an article I wrote in 2014. My goal was to identify seven troublesome editorial glitches that were not easily resolved. Here is the excerpt that tells all:

"Before 2014 ends, B2B editors could be addressing issues involving front cover integrity, ad contracts guaranteeing editorial staff assistance in writing ad copy, faulty fact-checking, increased supervision of marketing projects, unlabeled ads simulating regular editorial, need to create policy responding to requests to unpublish archived content, developing and posting of ethics guidelines.")

Ethics code clarifies marketing involvement

When the idea of the so-called church-and-state relationship between sales and editorial was all the rage, editorial staff participation in marketing activity was taboo. But the push from top management for editorial support for sales efforts gradually became the order of the day. Even so, editors remained concerned about crossing the integrity line. In its most recent ethics code, Guide to Best Practices, ASBPE recognized the need to define editorial-sales involvement limits:

> "A senior-level editor may work with sales personnel to ensure that no conflict exists between the advertiser-sponsored content and editorial content. Thus, the editor may suggest topics for the sponsor, but the publisher or the sales staff should be the ones to communicate these suggestions to the sponsor. (In other words, the editor should not directly communicate with the advertiser.) A publication's editorial staff should not write, edit, design, or lay out special advertising sections or supplements. This role should be handled by a freelancer hired by the sales staff or publisher or a separate non-editorial department."

More complicated in terms of imposing limits was participation by editors on joint presentation calls with sales personnel. The advisory ASBPE's ethics committee produced after considerable debate was more or less a compromise:

> "When editors are asked to accompany the publisher on an advertising visit, the occasion may be identified to all participants as an 'editorial call.' Agenda items may include discussing industry trends, explaining editorial policy and direction, or describing the readership. For any specific discussion of advertising matters, editors should not be present."

This advisory clearly requires amendment during the next ethics code revision. The key reason is the soaring popularity of sponsored content with an editorial flavor. In larger companies, this requirement is best fulfilled by a representative of the publisher's sponsored content department. In smaller firms, publishers should look to freelance writers who specialize in content marketing projects.

Despite the ASBPE advisory on the use of joint sales, it's

common for editors to trash the practice. Especially annoying are those cases where the call is dominated by a sales pitch, and the editor is there for window dressing. However, if the editor has the floor most of the time, the session usually is more productive. Even better perhaps is when the editor visits top brass on his or her own for interviews or to exchange views on industry trends. Of course, that editor will accomplish very little if only capable of providing low-value expertise.

Six unethical practices

In addition to the big-picture ethical issues reviewed above, editors also face ethical issues in their practice of the craft. Here are six that constantly require attention:

1. Inadequate fact-checking. Before online news made the scene, this practice already was a bad habit. A typical scenario found editors running controversial material published elsewhere without a preliminary accuracy check.

2. Fabrication. Typical abuse assumes the form of posting conjured quotes from anonymous sources. One reason this may happen is that the offender has been unsuccessful in building a list of reliable contacts.

3. Bad-news ban. This policy may originate with a publisher concerned about offending advertisers or prospects, even if the story in question should be told.

4. Blacklisting non-advertisers. When roundup articles are scheduled requiring vendor interviews, a publisher may create a priority list of contacts editors should ignore. This list may exclude industry sources having leadership positions in the product area being addressed.

5. Burying complaints. This happens when an editor is challenged by a source who alleges that his or her comments were reported inaccurately. Instead of dealing with the complaint, the editor takes no action, hoping the incident will die a quick death.

6. Plagiarism explosion. While this concern is well-documented, leading publishing authorities expect it to worsen. A key cause of this trend is mounting editorial workloads.

Integrity challenges vary widely

During my time on ASBPE's ethics committee, we received a number of inquiries from members about specific ethical challenges involving pressure from sales or marketing. The complexities involved are indicated by the headlines on some of our guidance statements:

- "Proactive marketing effort is editor's best response when publisher seeks to increase ad/editorial swaps."
- "Limits required when editor's participation in sponsored webinars is requested."
- "Be realistic when addressing sales department requests for stronger editorial hooks."

Let's take a closer look at excerpts from the advisory pertaining to editorial hooks. This is an especially troublesome issue, often the source of considerable negotiation when annual calendars are being prepared.

"Issue: Editors increasingly being pressed by salespeople to schedule articles that have 'advertiser appeal.' In some cases, the desired 'hooks' are not perceived to offer the highest reader value. To what extent can editors defend quality and ethics concerns without jeopardizing their careers?"

"Response: ASBPE's Guide to Preferred Editorial Practices stipulates that an editor has primary responsibility 'for selection of editorial content based on readers' needs and interests.' There is no question that maintaining editorial quality deserves the highest priority. However, a knee-jerk negative reaction to including hook material would be unrealistic. Actually, so-called hook content may have significant reader appeal. All it takes is an adept editor to fashion a high-quality article covering the subject in question."

The advisory continued by offering reactions and recommendations from six ethics committee members. At the time, I was committee chairman. Here is what I said:

"When considering the issue of selecting content based on advertiser value rather than reader value, there are cases where many topics offer equal value potential for both factions. Being an editor is truly a dream job on a B2B magazine serving such a field. On the other side of the coin, editors have good cause to despair when employed by publications where the mandate is to provide cover-to-cover hooks for advertisers. Unfortunately, there still are some of those around.

"Based on my experience as an editor, the best environment we can hope for is one where senior management accords top priority to editorial quality."

I concluded my remarks by reminding readers that "the preceding discussion occurred because a peer had the courage to initiate the conversation!"

APPENDIX

Tips for Better Editorial Content

Five keys to hiring efficiency

When it comes to hiring, at least five time-saving paths are worth traveling. If you have established realistic performance goals in terms of hours required per task that you can discuss with applicants, evaluation of their skills is more easily measured.

1. Always run want ads that include a specific salary or a narrow salary range. You certainly know what you can afford to pay, so why run an auction? Even when you are specific about salary, you'll still attract a certain percentage of negotiators.

2. Have a system for evaluating ad responses and stick to it. You may miss some winners along the way, but you'll also save a lot of time. My system includes first eliminating all responses not accompanied by a cover letter, then eliminating all responses with boilerplate cover letters, and last, evaluating the remaining responses with letter grades of A, B, and C. I then call the A group for interviews.

3. Be wary of applicants who say they want to return to editorial work after a career in sales or marketing and that they are willing to take a cut to get back in. Their claims are not always true. Some of them may be looking for a place to camp

until the right situation comes along. If you hire such a settler, you could be unsettled in the near future.

4. As noted in Chapter 2, a written test should be part of your screening process. The test should be objective enough that anyone can grade it. Include exercises covering grammatical skills, editing facility, headline writing, and news sense. But be aware that a written test may not cover all the skills you need. If a candidate promising in other ways flunks the exam, you may have to decide whether his or her other skills compensate for test shortcomings.

5. When interviewing candidates, have a predetermined list of checkpoints that will allow you to rate key attributes from 0 to 3, with 3 being best. This assessment will be especially useful as a tiebreaker when two or more finalists appear equally qualified for the position. As an example, here are the candidate checkpoints I have used:

- On time for interview
- Friendly greeting
- Evidence of productivity
- Organized portfolio
- Ability to relate past experience to position offered
- Photography skills
- Capable traveler
- Enthusiastic response to job described
- Dresses for success

- Previous job longevity

- Effective speaking and interviewing ability

- Strong test results

Nine suggestions for better headlines

Here's a refresher course covering nine ways to inject more story value into every headline and deck you write.

1. Include a high-impact number. It seems that B2B editors are not sufficiently tuned in to writing headlines with a quantitative flavor. I'm reminded of this problem every time I judge editorial awards competitions. In a collective group of, say, dozens of headlines, only a handful use numbers. Surprisingly, this shortcoming is most notable in research-oriented features that cry out for number-packed headlines. Sure, you don't always need to use a number. And sometimes numbers don't see the light of day because an article's author wasn't required to gather quantitative facts.

2. In place of one or two verb-less labels on magazine covers, use at least four or five active headlines.

3. Every contents page blurb should be treated as a headline + deck combination. Each blurb's objective is to sell reader value. Vague boldface heads accompanied by superficial blurbs will not do the trick. And try to avoid using only generic heads to identify departments.

4. Avoid redundant headlines and decks, where both elements essentially convey the same message.

5. Sometimes headlines using only three or four words have kicker value at best. In fact, too many headline writers are burdened by policies imposing limited word counts. Other times, too many attempts are made to be clever rather than informative.

6. The editor's personal column definitely requires a headline longer than a few words. When I judge competitions for best editorial column, I am impressed when a headline, deck, and callout are used to convey article value.

7. Interesting letters to the editor often are burdened by two- or three-word un-headlines. If this is a matter of policy at your publication, abandon it now.

8. High-value headlines describe what the writer discovered rather than what event he or she covered.

9. All captions should function as mini-headlines. Headshot photographs in a feature article, accompanied by two-word labels consisting of subject's first and last name, are not adequate.

Diversify your editorial calendar

When planning your annual editorial calendar, how much thought do you give to editorial diversity? During annual company-wide studies for some clients, I have identified as many as 30 possible editorial formats. Diversity-conscious editors will offer at least eight varieties per issue.

With the recent pressure from steadily increasing online workloads, thoughts of diversity have taken a back seat for many besieged editors. Don't let it happen to you! In the absence of variety, your publication or website becomes predictable, making you a sitting duck when your opposition runs its next competitive analysis study. Having said that, let's list five options that are usually standard practice for print and online formats:

- A high-benefit cover
- Timely letters to the editor
- An interesting last page
- A Q&A interview
- Original research

A high-benefit cover will offer four to five active headlines (no label headlines, please) describing key editorial content in the issue. Q&A interviews can be based on an extensive interview with one person, or the popular "X questions with _____" style.

Next we have 10 formats that will usually be used at least once during a calendar year:

- A mini-directory
- An innovative contents page
- Authoritative columnists
- A diary
- A supplement
- Case histories
- A step-by-step how-to photo sequence
- A handbook format
- A product award competition
- "Write for" information

Now we have my 10 favorites, many of which are prone to being delayed or cancelled because content development may be time consuming:

- A regular statistical column
- A problem-solution column
- A celebrity interview
- A mystery shopper article

- A point-counterpoint opinion piece
- Useful forms or diagrams
- A quiz
- An equipment field test review
- A day-in-the-life profile
- A roundtable discussion

Elaborate quizzes billed as industry IQ tests work especially well when challenging readers to demonstrate technical acumen. One magazine serving a financial audience regularly posted true-false and multiple-choice features that drew several hundred responses. An added benefit for the editor was the opportunity to schedule a cover story about test results, especially if most respondents flunked the exam. In one case, a client serving a retail field offered a dynamite article combining the mystery shopper and IQ test formats.

Rounding out my list of 30 ways to diversify are five formats that may justify an occasional appearance:

- A Who's Who special
- A book review section
- An information please or help desk column
- Humor
- A puzzle page

Finally, remember that wherever they are used, infographics enhance any diversity effort. Graphically speaking, many editors still fail to deliver infographics on the bare minimum of at least 20 percent of pages carrying editorial content.

Avoid 10 news shortfalls

When conducting news department management workshops, I rely on a training handout called "10 Common Hurdles that Defy Creation of a Hot News Section."

Here is a more detailed explanation of the pitfalls involved:

1. Total workload inhibits exclusivity. This problem is likely to plague smaller staffs, but the giants are not immune. Besieged editors feel lucky enough if they can assemble a routine section. However, some staffs have leeway to free-lance news assignments so that investigative coverage is guaranteed in each section. In some cases, B2B publishers have totally shut down any attempt to provide in-print news sections.

2. Prime reader group rarely quoted. In fact, some news sections only run quotes that obviously were lifted from press releases. In my studies of online news delivery, the absence of end-user sourced stories is the second biggest shortfall after lack of enterprise reporting.

3. 'Killer story' is missing. Even when the "obligatory news" load is overwhelming, schedule at least one socko article that counteracts the impression of humdrum reporting.

4. Minor items get major treatment. An effort to please advertisers usually is the cause of this shortfall. And in some cases, the result is online news or print packages that are nothing more than a collection of puff stuff. In online news in particular this practice clearly is getting out of hand. Why this has occurred stems from B2B's headlong plunge from weekly to daily newsletter frequency. Space must be filled no matter what, and that translates into individual articles jazzed up with big headline type and giant photos. This is most common with announcements of new products and personnel changes, where supposed "articles" are nothing but reproduction of PR announcements.

5. Major items get minor treatment. This factor can be an outgrowth of the previous point. For example, you have four pages of a five-page news section occupied by trivia. One possible solution: See how many minor blurbs can be boiled down even further. A good place to start: personnel items.

6. Headline skills need honing. Many news stories must struggle harder for reader attention because headlines consist of easily written but bland generalizations rather than idea-packed messages. Other aspects of news coverage—such as an overload of long-winded sentences—also need work. But headlines are the best place to start.

7. No room to maneuver. In the case of print media, tighter editorial budgets have produced space cutbacks that result in minimum allocation to news coverage.

8. Graphics format creates a "yawn" environment. All headlines are the same size, usually too small. Also missing: column-width variation, sidebars, screens, and colors.

9. Too many pages lack story-telling photos. This shortfall is a spin-off of the previous point. An overload of all-type pages will surely result if the editorial staff doesn't think through its illustration needs in advance. Sometimes the solution is as simple as requiring a graphics/page ratio. For example, ensure every page is illustrated and that at least 20 percent of those pages use infographics.

10. Long production times have gotten longer. Some editors of print monthlies face copy deadlines of up to 60 days before publication date. And as far as online news is concerned, it's the opposite problem: an emphasis on immediate posting frequently produces a run of embarrassing oversights.

Interview training must be challenging

Whether you conduct a workshop on interviewing technique for a group or just a single staff member, be sure the session is challenging. Don't just lecture for 30 to 45 minutes and call it a day. Engage attendees by encouraging participation during the class and requiring "homework" they must submit within the hour following your program.

My favorite approach involves a mock interview. In this scenario, the workshop leader plays the role of an evasive chief executive conducting a conference call focusing on the company's alleged slipshod performance. Attendees are required to ask tough questions designed to yield newsworthy details. After the session, the accumulated notes of the attendees are converted into a worthy article submitted for evaluation.

Your interviewing workshop also should cover a variety of interviewing techniques. One example is the value of "rehearsing" with a possible interviewee before setting a date for the actual interview. Let's say a query letter comes to one of our retail publications from a medium-size designing firm. "The president of our company has some fabulous ideas on how retailers can design cosmetic departments," promises the PR contact. "It would make a great interview; the president is really imaginative, speaks everywhere, is very creative, etc., etc. Let's have lunch to discuss the possibilities."

In this situation, I advise my editor to have a preliminary conversation directly with the PR person's client. Within 10 minutes, it becomes clear the source is a dud with nothing of value to say. Rehearsals may not have a negative outcome every time. But it pays to test the waters.

Here's another approach: If time allows—or perhaps in a

follow-up session—review possible solutions to typical situations that often baffle inexperienced interviewers. Use these questions to get the session rolling:

1. You secure an appointment with a hospital administrator on the subject of how operating costs were reduced 15 percent without cuts in services available to patients. You arrived at the executive's office promptly and are kept waiting for 20 minutes. Finally, you get in to see this individual. After the preliminaries, you're ready to start firing questions. What's the first one?

2. You are conducting a series of interviews for a roundup article. What is the best procedure for making sure each individual interview is more effective than the previous one?

3. When you are taking notes, does the size of the notepad you use influence your ability to keep up with the response? How about whether the pad is lined or unlined?

4. What are the advantages and disadvantages of taping a detailed Q&A?

5. What are good sources to consult before an interview with a highly publicized source?

Here are possible answers to each of the above questions:

1. If an editor arrives on time for an interview and is kept waiting for 20 minutes or more, the interviewee may have less time to respond to questions. So what you need to know immediately is "are we still good for an hour's discussion?" (or words to that effect). If the allocated time has been squeezed to 30 or 40 minutes, reorganize your planned sequence of questions so that all or most of your top inquiries are covered.

2. As each interview is concluded, transfer notes to a more readable form. Studying coverage as you go along may suggest that a key topic has been covered sufficiently. You may not need to interview any more sources.

3. When taking notes, never use an unlined pad. Instead, use a pad with the smallest possible space between lines. This will force you to WRITE SMALL. As a result, you'll be better able to keep up with your source. I learned this lesson years ago while taking a course in Morse code. Training exercises included converting transmitted dashes and dots into letters at gradually increasing speeds. The smaller you transcribed, the better.

4. For some editors, the key hurdle when using a tape recorder is transcribing. If you have someone else doing this for you, it would be a big time-saver. Otherwise, you could spend an awesome stretch replaying comments. I never use a tape recorder—even for the longest Q&A interviews. Writing small—as noted above—works for me!

5. In today's computer age, using your favorite search engine allows you to research interviewees in a jiffy. Pay special attention to the quality of information conveyed by your upcoming source during interviews with competitive publications.

No matter what the circumstances, be sure your workshop covers the importance of preparing one or more lists of questions. One of those lists should require numeric answers. A good homework assignment for your training seminar is to require attendees to submit sample lists of questions for your review and feedback.

Assignment editors must provide clear objectives to staff editors

You'd think the preference for clarity would be a no-brainer for assigning editors. But in today's environment of work overload, nothing can be assumed. During a recent project focusing on online news improvement, I found evidence that assignments were being made hastily. Adequate direction on story angles and contacts was lacking. If you're guilty of this error, you are placing inexperienced junior editors in a quandary. No matter how valiant an effort they make to gather information, the story is likely to fall short. What's more, the assignee usually ends up being criticized unjustly for failing to deliver the goods.

The solution I proposed was to insist that a more adequate approach to story assignment be used. The new system required three parties—the editor-in-chief, the managing editor, and the editorial consultant (me)—serving as coaches for subordinate staff. Here's how the revised assignment system worked:

The editor-in-chief passed along press releases and similar materials for assistant editors to write up. Instructions included placement recommendations regarding channels, resources, research, etc. Additionally, the staff editor would be told which releases should be pursued for enterprise reporting, and given suggestions for potential sources.

Before writing the article, the staff editor would further discuss the goals with the managing editor to identify specific subject matter to report, to nail down sources, and to draft specific questions.

The staff editor would then complete the first draft and send the file to the consultant for analysis and tutoring. Based on the consultant's feedback, the staff editor would make revisions as necessary, and send the file to managing editor. Finally, the editor-in-chief would review the completed article, including headline and presentation elements.

The above procedure may seem routine, but my ongoing online news reviews suggest it's not happening. As one publisher recently explained: "With the load of content we generate daily, there no longer is time to assign or deliver articles that meet our standards."

How to maximize editorial board feedback

Forming and overseeing an editorial advisory board is a time-consuming process. For that reason, many editors put it off. They shouldn't. Once you have an authoritative, dedicated group of board members in place, the benefits for your editorial content can be significant.

Here are four possible ways to get maximum input from board members:

1. Send published articles to selected members for comment.

2. Use a peer-review board to recommend improvements for articles prior to publication.

3. Poll the group twice a year (I prefer telephone as opposed to impersonal e-mail surveys or snail mail).

4. Host a classy dinner during a major convention that most board members are likely to attend.

Of the above tactics, the last two are the most promising. When polling board members, I usually draw up a list of 10 questions I wish to discuss with them. The objective is not so much to get feedback on past issues as to determine what we should be doing next. I also seek board member perceptions on how they rank us against the competition in terms of editorial strengths and weaknesses. One of my key concerns is whether other magazines or websites are doing a better job than we of maintaining personal relationships with board members.

Once my list is ready, I send a letter to each board member outlining the agenda. I ask for 30 minutes of their time and to expect my call shortly to set up a date for a telephone interview. When board members are first recruited, they are advised that these interviews are a condition of board participation.

As for organizing a board, it helps if you've already established contact with many of the executives you'd like to join your group. (The number of board members is typically limited to 25.) Your invitation should outline membership benefits. In my case, I was able to offer exclusive information alerts that would be available to board members. Another perk was the availability of a qualified staff member to provide a special briefing to a board member's executive group on current industry trends. Also worth mentioning are the usual benefits, like being listed on the magazine's masthead and receiving a handsome plaque as recognition for service.

Last but not least, if your arrangement is working smoothly, you should be able to interview board members occasionally for a high-value, exclusive feature to appear in your magazine or website.

For many editors, brevity remains a foreign language

Be brief! That's the focus of most search engine advisories that address writing for websites. Use short sentences and short paragraphs. Ledes should make important points within the first few words. And don't let vocabulary get out of control.

Following this advice should be duck soup for most editors. But that's hardly the case. On the web—and in magazines too—long-winded writing lives on. Parades of endless sentences are the rule rather than the exception. And here's a puzzling thing: In some cases where a magazine's news section is appropriately fast-paced, website copy written by the same staff is plodding.

Why does this happen? Any seasoned editor reviewing submitted copy should immediately see that 40-word sentence sequences need deflating. Since a lot of news material has the flavor of press release rewrite, perhaps time pressure discourages necessary revision. And how about those puffy quotes often included in merger announcements, financial results, appointments, and other corporate news releases? Why do we let many platitudes buried therein escape the editorial axe?

Rather than rave further, here is my list of seven pitfalls that inevitably subject readers to long-sentence fatigue. If you avoid these bad habits, your endless-sentence disease may vanish:

1. The first sentence of article is too long, exceeding 25 to 30 words. The reason: information overload.

2. Event identification and location lumped together requires too many words.

3. Basic, long compound sentences are not immediately split during the editing process. Is there any excuse for that?

4. A long introductory clause traps the author into writing an even longer sentence.

5. Press release babble, especially when housed in long quotes, is allowed to survive unedited. We must plead with PR contacts to simplify their quote selection.

6. A sentence involving a direct quote includes the source's name, company, and title (which

may be a mouthful). A better way is to split the attribution so that the person's name and company name appear in one sentence. The full title (often overly long) appears in the next sentence.

7. Finally, some advice about the need for "speedy" ledes. Take a hard look at your website and magazine news intros. How many words appear before a key story point is made? I still see too many ledes where 20 or 30 words are expended before the real story starts. Our goal for ledes nowadays, especially for online news, must be no more than five words before getting to the point.

Using Fog Index analysis

Every tutorial on writing for the Web that I've reviewed stresses the importance of brevity. But clearly that message has not registered with many B2B editors. Fortunately, there are several formulas at hand for achieving tighter writing. My favorite always has been the Fog Index.

I learned about the Fog Index in my first B2B job as an assistant editor. The editorial director of the company required all new staff to read *The Technique of Clear Writing* by Robert Gunning. This book explained how to find levels of reading difficulty using a measure Gunning named the Fog Index. His system helped writers produce prose at a grade level that readers could easily absorb. (Though no longer in print, used copies of Gunning's book are for sale on many websites. For instance, Amazon lists a hardback version "from $3.00.")

The Fog Index premise is that an acceptable writing level falls somewhere between 10th and 12th grade. You can find the grade level by taking a passage of roughly 100 words and performing the following calculations:

1. Determine the average sentence length.

2. Count the number of "hard words" (that is, words of three or more syllables, excluding proper names). Divide the number by the total number of words and multiply by 100 to find the hard-word percentage.

3. Add the numbers for average sentence length and hard-word percentage. Multiply the result by 0.4.

4. Drop any decimals from the resulting number. This produces the grade level of the passage.

As an example, let's analyze the second paragraph of this section (the one beginning with "I learned about...").

1. It is 93 words long with six sentences, for an average sentence length of 16.

2. It includes 7 hard words, for a hard-word percentage of 8 (7 divided by 93).

3. Adding the average sentence length (16) and the hard-word percentage (8) results in 24. Multiplying 24 by 0.4 results in 9.6.

4. Drop the decimal to come up with a grade level of 9.

My basics workshop always offers a Fog Index exercise. But one of the best examples I've seen comes from a webinar developed by consultant John Bethune while he was editorial VP for a medical publisher. Apply your defogging skills now to the following passage:

Foggy Version

"Against a backdrop of ongoing discussions at the European level on the prevention of nosocomial infections, the report stressed that only disposable products are able to provide an adequate degree of protection in the operating theater. Medical personnel have joined the crusade, citing the unreliability of traditional sterilization techniques to protect them from exposure to Creutzfeldt-Jakob disease and H.I.V. Healthcare workers have formed committees in France and other European countries with the aim of identifying and eliminating these and other sources of infection."

Help! This 86-word mammoth includes 18 "hard" words (21 percent) and three sentences (average sentence length = 29 words). Adding 21 and 29 and multiplying the total of 50 by 0.4 shows that the writer has buried the reader in 20th grade-level writing.

Defogged Version

"Preventing nosocomial infection has been an urgent, ongoing topic at the highest levels in Europe. The report's finding that only disposable products can ensure the safety of drapes and gowns will heighten the debate. Medical staffs have already joined the crusade against reuse. Reused products, they say, even when sterilized, cannot protect them from exposure to Creutzfeldt-Jakob disease and H.I.V. In France and other European countries, they have formed committees to find and wipe out these and other sources of infection."

In this simplified version, we have 84 total words, 9 hard words (10 percent), and 5 sentences (average sentence length of 17). The Fog Index grade level is now a more digestible 10.

Acknowledgements

I am grateful to long-time friend and associate John Bethune, himself a B2B editorial management veteran, for his advice in the development of this book. As the principal of ReefNet Press, he also played a major role in the editing, formatting, and publication of this book.

About the Author

Howard S. Rauch is president of Editorial Solutions Inc., a business-to-business consulting firm he launched in 1989. Since then, he has worked with publishing clients on a variety of editorial management assignments. His special interests include competitive analysis, editorial productivity measurement, and, more recently, online news quality.

In 2012 he published his first book, *Get Serious About Competitive Editorial Analysis*. It provides a detailed review of how to apply quantitative assessment of qualitative factors pertaining to news, features, graphics, debut issues, and trade show coverage.

Before founding his consultancy, Howard spent 21 years with leading trade publisher Gralla Publications, the last 13 as vice president and editorial director. Among other Gralla accomplishments, he developed an extensive in-house training program involving several dozen workshops directed to various editorial management levels.

Howard recently completed two terms as ethics committee chairman for the American Society of Business Publication Editors (ASBPE). He now serves as news editor of ASBPE'S quarterly ethics newsletter. In 2002, he was the recipient of ASBPE's Lifetime Achievement Award.

Connect with Howard online:

Business e-mail:	editsol1@optimum.net
ASBPE e-mail:	fogindex12@gmail.com
Website:	www.editsol.com
Twitter:	www.twitter.com/editsol
LinkedIn:	www.linkedin.com/in/editsol

Made in the USA
San Bernardino, CA
21 August 2017